Teach Your Child
How to Learn

Teach Your Child How to Learn

*Fun ways to give your child
a good start in life*

SU GARNETT

howtobooks

Published by How To Books Ltd,
3 Newtec Place, Magdalen Road,
Oxford OX4 1RE. United Kingdom.
Tel: (01865) 793806. Fax: (01865) 248780.
email: info@howtobooks.co.uk
http://www.howtobooks.co.uk

First edition 2002

British Library Cataloguing in Publication Data.
A catalogue record for this book is available from
the British Library.

Cartoons by John Betts
Cover design by Baseline Arts Ltd, Oxford

Produced for How To Books by Deer Park Productions
Typeset by PDQ Typesetting, Newcastle-under-Lyme, Staffs.
Printed and bound by Cromwell Press, Trowbridge, Wiltshire

NOTE: The material contained in this book is set out in good
faith for general guidance and no liability can be accepted
for loss or expense incurred as a result of relying in particular
circumstances on statements made in the book. Laws and
regulations are complex and liable to change, and readers should
check the current position with the relevant authorities before
making personal arrangements.

Contents

Preface

Every parent wants their child to do well at school and to reach their full potential. We continue to learn all the time, throughout the whole of our lives and if our children are to make the most of this learning, we need to encourage them to become effective learners at an early stage. This book is designed to help you help your child to develop the necessary skills.

The book does not tell you how to help your child learn to read, spell or do maths. Rather, it suggests how you can help him to acquire learning skills in general. These will help him to make the most of every learning opportunity. The book is full of ideas and activities for stimulating your child, using everyday situations. You will be teaching him to think, to observe and to ask questions. When a child enjoys discovering and learning in this way, then any form of education or experience at any time in his life will be fruitful.

It is fully recognised that none of us seem to have enough time to do all the things we want to nowadays. Parents live very busy lives and are often trying to juggle work and home life. This book shows that teaching your child how to learn does not need to take an enormous amount of extra time. Everyday experiences and activities provide excellent opportunities to aid the learning process. As you rush around, doing all the normal things that people do, it is so easy to take familiar sights and experiences for granted. If you stop to look further, there are so many possibilities for stimulating and exciting your child and making him keen to learn more. By talking to your child, showing him things and asking him questions, you can encourage an early interest in learning. Holidays, when you can be more relaxed, also provide the perfect opportunity to develop and extend this learning.

To learn effectively, children need an enquiring mind and a genuine curiosity. Most children are naturally curious. They want to learn and are usually enthusiastic about what they are able to find out. It is therefore very easy to develop these natural talents by pointing out things they may not have noticed before and by asking the sort of questions that encourage them to think about what they have seen. As they absorb information, they are bound to ask for clarification. It is then your role to listen carefully and to try to respond helpfully. At times, the everlasting 'why?' can seem monotonous, but it is a trait to be encouraged! Much of this book is dedicated to encouraging you and your child to notice and think about new aspects of familiar surroundings, by pointing out and questioning in this way.

Other chapters include activities to extend a child's newly acquired understanding and to develop his imagination. Reinforcing a child's new learning with practical activities helps him to understand new concepts much more quickly, which makes him highly motivated to learn. Exciting practical activities are also a very good way to increase your child's ability to concentrate.

The more a child feels he understands about his world, the more confident he will feel within it. Therefore, all these activities are also very helpful in building confidence.

The emphasis of the book is very firmly on fun. If anything ceases to be fun and becomes a chore, you are getting a very clear signal from your child that he has had enough. Back off for a while and take his lead as to when he might be ready for more.

A NOTE ON LANGUAGE

Throughout the text, for ease of use, I have referred to your child as 'he'. All thoughts and suggestions are equally valid for both sexes. In addition, any reference to parents clearly refers to both mothers and fathers and may well be of interest and use to grandparents and others who care for young children.

In later chapters, reference is made to all kinds of workers and the jobs they do. It is fully recognised that all jobs may be carried out by both men and women and any reference to gender refers equally to both men and women.

ACKNOWLEDGEMENTS

I would like to thank my own children, Lucy, Emma and Simon and all the young children I have taught over the years for inspiring and exciting me with their enthusiasm and interest for everything around them. May my first grandson, Harry, find the exploration of his world as fascinating.

Su Garnett

1

Learning Skills

One of the most important things for a child to realise is that he is not the only one who is learning. Everyone continues to learn throughout the whole of their lives. We learn from observing and discussing. We learn from experimenting. We learn from our mistakes and from the mistakes of others. If we are enthusiastic and interested in life, we will learn from our everyday experiences. If we are curious about things and determined to find out more, we will find the necessary motivation to continue in our quest for knowledge.

Our first teachers are usually our parents and those who look after us when we are very young. Therefore, they are the ones who have the first and most important impact on a child's future attitudes to learning. They also have the first opportunities to encourage the development of the essential skills which help anyone, at whatever stage in their lives, to learn effectively.

Children begin to learn at a very early age by responding to different sights and sounds. Consider the very young baby who looks carefully at the face in front of him, smiling at a familiar one and possibly crying at one he does not recognise. He will respond in a similar way to familiar and unfamiliar sounds. As he grows up, he brings his other senses into play, deciding what he does and does not like to taste and touching everything in sight with both his fingers and his tongue. Use of the senses is clearly extremely important as children start the learning process and in the development of that process. The next chapter is dedicated to helping children to develop all five senses.

When children are older and are able to get around freely and communicate reasonably well, they become increasingly aware of what is going on around them. It is at this stage that it becomes particularly important to harness that inquisitiveness and encourage children to look very carefully at everything. Chapter 3 is concerned with developing good observation skills.

ESSENTIAL LEARNING SKILLS

Children embarking on the learning process need to acquire a number of different skills. Some are part of most children's make-up – their natural talents – while others need to be encouraged and developed. While it is very important to encourage your child to develop these skills, it is also very important not to overwhelm him. Always remember to take the lead from him and be sensitive to when he has had enough. It is easy to slip into the trap of always answering a question with another question, in the firm belief that you are helping your child by so doing. You may well be, but sometimes it is necessary to give him a straight answer. Just as you may find it exhausting to be stimulated all the time, so may your child. I am reminded of watching my new grandson who loves being talked to and stimulated with bright toys. He gurgles and smiles and moves his limbs excitedly for quite some time. Then, suddenly, just as quickly as he appeared to be 'turned on', he suddenly 'switches off' and falls into a deep sleep. Endless stimulation and concentration is clearly an exhausting business!

What are these essential skills?
- **Curiosity and a desire to explore further**. Most children have an innate curiosity and want to know all about everything. A questioning attitude and an enquiring mind are both essential to successful learning. It is very difficult for a child to enjoy learning if he is not curious about the things around him and does not have a will to know more. Therefore encouragement of this natural curiosity is vital because it will lead to greater understanding.

- **Alertness and awareness**. It is essential for children to be aware of what is going on around them, for their own safety and for that of others. They will miss out on much knowledge if they are not receptive to new ideas and experiences.

- **Careful and logical thought**. Young children are very impetuous and often tend to do things without thinking about the consequences of their actions. Not many children will be deterred from jumping into that glorious puddle because they might get wet and muddy feet. If they want something someone else has got, their immediate reaction will often be to snatch it away. There is a great tendency to think they know something already, which can lead to a reluctance to think more deeply about something. Consider trying to dress independently or learning how to hold a knife and fork properly to cut up food. If your child does not give the task careful thought, he will end up with both his legs inside one trouser leg or with his food on the floor! Careful, logical thought also increases a child's ability to be able to reason and to predict what will happen.

- **Discussion skills – communicating and listening – memory**. To make the most of new learning experiences, children need to be able to ask questions, listen to answers and ask follow-up questions, which can lead to a productive discussion. The more they are exposed to situations which make them think, the easier they will find this. To encourage listening skills and to help your child to understand and remember, it is very important to give simple, clear explanations. Try to link new experiences to existing knowledge wherever possible, for example, describing a ship's anchor in terms of a dog lead which prevents a dog from running away from its owner. It is also important for children to speak for themselves at every opportunity if they are to be able to develop good discussion skills.

- **Imagination**. A vivid imagination will help your child to be creative and to fully appreciate literature, art and music.

How can you help your child to develop these important learning skills?

The following chapters suggest how you can encourage development of these skills by making the most of everyday experiences as you go out and about and as you do your everyday tasks. You will be encouraging your child to look at the world in a new light, noticing more and more and thinking again about familiar experiences. You will also be developing his imaginative skills. By asking questions about why things are happening, you will be introducing your child to the idea of discussing ideas, contributing thoughts and listening carefully to explanations. Your aim is to get to a position where your child is pointing things out to you, rather than the other way round. He will then have become very aware of everything that is going on around him and will be keen to show you what he has noticed. If you have managed to excite him to the stage where he wants to know why things are the way they are or why and how things happen, you will have put him well on the way towards effective learning.

What are the likely results of developing these learning skills?

- **Enthusiasm for and an interest in a wide variety of things**. Most young children are very enthusiastic. However, as they grow older, they can become cynical. By showing children more and more to be interested in, you will hopefully maintain this enthusiasm.

- **Growing confidence and independence**. Confidence grows when your child feels a success. Understanding something new or completing a task successfully gives your child a tremendous feeling of satisfaction, reinforces confidence and encourages him to have another go. There is nothing like success to fuel future success.

- **Motivation and perseverance**. Children need to feel motivated in order to want to learn how to do things. By discussing and explaining experiences as described and by opening up possibilities for learning, you will help them to find the necessary motivation.

- **Concentration**. Learning anything new takes time and effort and careful concentration is essential. Consider trying to learn how to ride a bike for the first time. You have to be able to balance on two narrow wheels, control both your feet on the pedals, steer and keep a careful lookout all at the same time. If you begin to think about something else, you are immediately in trouble and start to wobble as a prelude to falling off! Now think about learning how to write. You have to hold the pencil correctly, remember where to start writing and in which direction, where to begin writing individual letters and what you want to say – again, all at once. Without concentration, you are lost! Developing concentration is a slow process as young children can only concentrate for a short time on a formal task. The beauty of this 'everyday situation' learning is that children are concentrating and thinking, often without really realising it. You will be developing concentration naturally.

2

Using the Senses

Careful use of the senses is of enormous value when trying
to understand the world. Without thinking, we all use our
senses all the time. What are these senses?

- sight
- hearing
- touch
- smell
- taste.

Without the ability to use these senses, we are severely
hampered and have to rely heavily on other aids (guide
dogs, Braille, hearing aids) to get us through life. However,
a loss of one of the senses can make the others much more
acute because of an increased reliance on that particular
sense. This indicates that anyone can develop their senses by
careful concentration on them.

WHY ARE THE SENSES IMPORTANT IN HELPING YOUR CHILD TO LEARN?

For young children, the world must seem a very complex
and strange place. They have very limited experiences and
everything is new and potentially frightening. To change this
fear into curiosity and excitement, children need to be
helped to understand what is going on – what is possibly a
threat and what is completely natural. This is where the
senses come in as an invaluable aid. This is particularly true
for children whose speech is limited when very young and

who cannot express themselves clearly or understand other people's explanations.

EXPLAINING THE SENSES TO YOUNG CHILDREN

Activities

Looking at their bodies
Start by showing your child what various parts of his body do, in order for him to understand that while movements are related to legs, arms and joints, the senses are related to eyes, ears, finger tips, noses and tongues. Encourage him to join in, by playing a game such as 'Simon says'. This will help him to realise which part of his body he is using to copy your movements.

- *Parts which make you move – legs and arms*
  Walk slowly backwards and forwards, run on the spot, wave and clap.

- *Other parts which make you bend and move – knee, elbow, spine*
  Kneel down, pretend to shake hands with someone and curl up in a ball.

- *The part which makes you see*
  Wink with one eye and blink with two.

- *The part which makes you hear*
  Pretend to be 'cupping' your ear in order to hear.

- *The part with which you can touch*
  Tap the table lightly with finger tips, pretend to stroke a cat's fur, pretend to be walking in sticky mud.

- *The part with which you can smell*
  Pretend to be smelling a rose; hold your nose as you pretend to smell an unpleasant smell.

- *The part with which you can taste*
  Stick your tongue out and try to touch your nose with
  the tip of your tongue.

Playing other games

1. **Seeing games**
   Gather together a few objects which are each big enough
   to be partially covered with a cloth, such as a tray, a
   book, a cardigan, a sock, a fork, a mug and so on.
   Before playing the game, partially cover each object so
   that it is not too easily identified and then ask your child
   to guess what each object is just by looking at the part
   he can see.

   Put a large collection of different objects together on a
   tray so that they are arranged in a fairly random manner
   and partially cover one another. Know what the objects
   are and how many you have and then ask your child to
   identify as many as he can without moving anything on
   the tray.

2. **Hearing game**
   Stand behind your child, or if you know that the
   temptation to turn around will be too strong, blindfold
   him and make several noises, in turn, for him to identify.
   Simple sounds include a baby's rattle, a bell, the jingling
   of coins, tearing paper, brushing the floor, a tap running
   and so on.

3. **Blindfold game for the sense of touch**
   Collect a few simple objects, such as a teaspoon, a toy
   brick, a blunt pencil, a child's pair of scissors, an apple,
   a ball, a book and so on. Blindfold your child, using a
   loose scarf and hand him one of the objects. Can he tell
   you what it is just by feeling it?

4. **Blindfold game for the sense of smell**
   Collect together a few objects with strong and familiar
   smells, such as soap, a rose, chocolate, a lemon, etc.

Again, blindfold your child and ask him to identify each smell in turn while you hold the object under his nose.

5. **Blindfold game for the sense of taste**
    Provide a few, easily identifiable tastes that you know your child will enjoy. Again, using the blindfold, encourage him to try each taste and tell you what it is. Try to provide some sweet and some savoury tastes.

Having played these games on a number of occasions, your child should be fairly familiar with what it means to use his senses and, consequently, receptive to how this knowledge can help him become more aware.

DEVELOPING AWARENESS

Helping a child to be more aware of what is going on around him is very helpful in helping him to acquire general learning skills. Being aware is the cornerstone to all learning. It leads to a growing curiosity and a desire to find out more.

An initial concentration on the senses is an appropriate and easy way to introduce young children to the world and all it has to offer. Careful explanations will have their place later on, but it is much easier for a young child to learn by actively using parts of his body to explore what is happening. By concentrating carefully on the senses, children can be encouraged to become increasingly aware of the delights, peculiarities and dangers that surround them.

This will lead to a greater understanding of what things mean and of how they should respond in different circumstances. The delights of the world are there to be enjoyed but when their senses are alerted to peculiarities, there is generally an interesting reason for it. The reason could suggest that they should be cautious or it could just be a new learning opportunity. When their senses tell them that something is completely out of the ordinary, this generally indicates danger and the need to react immediately to avert disaster.

Familiarity

Very young children feel comfortable and are able to relax when they are familiar with the people looking after them, their surroundings and what is happening to them. They respond to a regular routine. This will not be the same for any one family or indeed for any one child. However, it is a routine which will have been established and one which will allow children to know where they are. At this very young age, many children feel threatened by any disruption to this familiar pattern.

Obviously, however, as children get older, they need to be able to cope with changes to this familiarity. They need to learn to accept many unfamiliar places, people, situations and objects as non-threatening, whilst recognising that some others pose a threat. As children become more adept at using their senses, their familiar world will expand dramatically and they will gradually develop a more realistic view of what is and what is not safe.

To begin the learning process, they need to notice, enjoy and become familiar with a huge variety of different things.

DELIGHTS

As adults, we regularly use our senses to enhance our enjoyment of so many things. Children need to be encouraged to do the same, thus increasing their ability to get the most out of all the delights that life offers.

Sight

As they grow up, children need to be encouraged to look carefully at their surroundings so they notice more and more detail.

Colour

At first, young children tend to think in terms of simple colours – blue, green etc. – without distinguishing between different shades and hues. Most will be able to identify different colours but will not readily think beyond that.

They need encouragement and practice to be able to distinguish and appreciate different shades.

Activity – Provide children with a small pot of white and black poster paint, two pots of paint in a primary colour of your choice, three small paintbrushes – one for each colour – several sheets of paper, a mixing palette and a jar of water. Help them to think about different shades of colour by challenging them to make as many different shades as they can by adding progressively, white paint and black paint. Start by painting a patch of pure colour on the paper. Then add a small amount of white paint to the pure colour, mix carefully and paint another patch on the paper. Continue to mix in white paint in this way and paint patches until the original colour has become very pale. Now start with a fresh pot of pure colour and paint patches for additions of black paint. At the end of the activity, you should have a complete range of colour from very pale to very dark. Promote further understanding by asking them questions to use this new-found knowledge. For example: How many different greens can they see in the garden? Is the sky the same bright blue as it was yesterday?

Views, flowers and animals
As adults, we are used to seeing different views. Children need to be shown different environments and they need to have features of each environment pointed out to them.

Activity – Use every opportunity to take your children to new places and make sure you point out the main features of each new environment. For instance, when you go for a walk in the country, talk about the hills, the woods, the lanes, wild flowers, the fields, farm and domestic animals, the sky and clouds. When you visit the seaside, notice waves, sand, smooth pebbles, seagulls and boats. When you go into a town, look out for traffic, shops, traffic lights, zebra crossings and so on. Encourage open discussion and help them to see the beauty in all these environments. Reinforce this at home, with the use of pictures and photographs.

Hearing

It is very easy, especially in a world which is increasingly dominated by canned music and extraneous noise, not to listen properly and children need to be encouraged to listen actively.

Music

Activity – Make sure children have the opportunity to listen to a wide variety of music. Avoid loud background music, but choose specific pieces of music to enjoy with your child at specific moments during the day. Obviously, what you choose to play will be governed largely by what you enjoy yourself, but try to choose a selection of as many types of music as you can, thus allowing your child to express likes and dislikes as well. You might choose rousing, energetic music at the start of the day and gentle, soothing music before he goes to sleep at night. Encourage movement to the music as a way of expressing himself. As he listens to the music, what does it make him think about? Encourage him to tell you whether or not he likes this music and why.

Bird song and the noises of nature

Activity – Go with your child into the park or garden. Sit together, close your eyes and listen carefully for the sounds of birds singing, leaves rustling, water gurgling, dogs barking and so on. See who can hear the most different sounds.

The human voice

It is vital that children get used to listening intently to the human voice, in all its variations, regardless of how softly people are speaking. Learning to recognise different voices and identifying different tones is a good indicator of safe or worrying situations.

Activity – Play games such as Chinese Whispers which involve whispering and very careful listening and repeating of what is heard. Read stories to your child in as animated and expressive voice as you can in order to introduce him to the delights of listening to the human voice.

Touch
The sense of touch reinforces delights which we can see. For instance, stroking a cat's gleaming fur greatly adds to the pleasure as does pulling on a soft, warm jumper on a chilly day. Swimming in cool water when we are very hot in the summer is lovely.

Activity – Play a game which involves guessing what something will feel like just by looking at it. Can children identify what will be cold/warm, rough/smooth, sticky/ prickly from sight alone?

Smell
Imagine a world without smells and you can quickly appreciate how important the sense of smell is to our overall enjoyment of life.

Activity – Help your child to appreciate pleasant smells by encouraging him to sniff flowers in the garden. Take him into shops where the smell of soap and cosmetics or flowers or chocolate is evident and encourage him to help you in the kitchen while you are cooking.

Taste
When your sense of taste is removed, perhaps because of a heavy cold, life becomes very boring and all food tastes the same. To develop a taste for certain foods and to appreciate good cooking, it is necessary to have taste buds working.

Activity – Play a game which requires your child to identify sweet from savoury food. Which does he like best?

By using the activities above, you will quickly encourage the development of your child's five senses. Now that he has become aware of how his senses can help him further his enjoyment, he is ready to move on and become aware of how his senses can help to warn him when something is different and he may need to be wary.

PECULIARITIES

You will need to point out these differences to your child, because, whilst we are very familiar with these sorts of changes, he will not necessarily notice them unless his attention is drawn to them.

Sight

- Food which is the wrong colour can indicate it is not fit to be eaten – green potatoes, black bananas, mouldy cheese.

- White frost on pavements can indicate a slippery surface which could be dangerous.

- An angry face, when it is usually friendly, can indicate trouble to come.

- Red spots on a usually clear skin may indicate illness.

- Seeing things from odd angles or in failing light can cause them to look different and unfamiliar and therefore threatening.

Activity – Involve your child in checking the freshness of food by looking at it carefully. Ask your child to describe something he has noticed which seems to him to be out of the ordinary and discuss it.

Hearing

- Unexpected, unfamiliar noises – crashes, cracks and bangs – can indicate that something is wrong, possibly falls and breakages.

- Unexpected silence can also be indicative of trouble!

Activity – Let your child see what has caused an unusual noise, perhaps a dropped plate or a slammed door.

Touch

- Sticky, prickly or stinging plants warn children against touching those plants again.

- Rough skin, when it is usually smooth, can indicate a skin problem and the need for some medication.

Activity – If your child has a younger sibling, let him help with nappy changes and so on. Most babies suffer some periods of nappy rash or rough skin. Let your child see the change from a normal clear skin and let him see what you are doing about it to make it better.

Smell

- Rotting food will give off a horrid smell to warn the potential consumer.

..leave a cabbage and a slice of bread to go mouldy and smelly and let your child see the results.

- Unpleasant body smells indicate the need for a nappy change or a bath!

Activity – If you can bear it, leave a cabbage and a slice of bread to go mouldy and smelly and let your child see the results of doing this.

Taste

- New foods will taste unfamiliar and warn the child of change, which he may or may not accept.

- A dry mouth can indicate illness.

Activity – Make sure your child has the opportunity to try lots of new food, if only to reject it – hopefully only initially!

DANGERS

Peculiarities noticed by the senses give us warning signs, but sometimes the senses give us a more urgent message of imminent danger.

Sight
- Fire or smoke should put us immediately on our guard.
- Crossing the road amongst busy traffic requires great care.
- Suspicious characters lurking where we would not expect them to be can be an indication of danger.

Activity – Teach your child how to cross the road safely by holding his hand and using the Green Cross Code.

Hearing
- Cars and lorries roaring down the road.
- Breaking glass.
- Screams.

Activity – Try to make your child understand that loud screams should be reserved for emergencies. Read them a 'Cry Wolf' story and explain the danger of people ignoring frequent screams.

Touch
- Objects which are too hot or cold will be quickly dropped.
- A sharp object pricks or cuts the skin, warning its holder to leave it immediately.

Activity – Take this opportunity to talk about safety in the home and to point out obvious dangers – fires, ovens, hobs, knives etc.

Smell

- Burning smells warn of fire danger.

Activity – Talk about the dangers of fire. Make sure your child can identify a burning smell. Under careful supervision and from a safe distance, let them smell a candle burning, bonfire smoke or burnt toast.

Taste

- Food which is off will taste horrible.

- Things which are not to be eaten will not normally pass the taste bud test – a warning taste will indicate that something is wrong.

- Very hot things are very quickly rejected by the taste buds.

Activity – Warn your child to let food cool down before he tries to eat it.

Be aware that any dangers your child has directly experienced may well have had a rather traumatic effect on him. Remember to comfort and reassure him, while at the same time, reinforcing how helpful it was that our senses told us about the danger.

SUMMARY

To understand new situations completely and to be aware of potential dangers, a child needs to be able to explore, using all five senses – sight, hearing, touch, smell and taste. Concentration on developing his ability to use his senses will increase his awareness. This, in turn, will help him to acquire learning skills in general.

3

Observation Skills

The purpose of this chapter is to encourage your child's observation skills and, using the evidence before him, to develop his ability to think about what might have caused certain phenomena. You are not required to give detailed scientific explanations! The world is full of wonderful things and children benefit from taking the time to look carefully at them and from considering why they are as magical as they look.

SEASIDE

Waves and spume

On windy days, on exposed beaches, you will be able to see huge waves out to sea and breaking on the shore. Point out the undersides of the waves as they break.They will often look quite yellow as they pick up the sand on sandy shores. Notice how quickly the breaking waves come in, ending with a frothy cream that races up the shore.

Activity – When you are exploring beaches at low tide, remind children how important it is to keep an eye on the tide coming in. Where beaches are flat, it can approach faster than an adult can walk, making these beaches potentially quite dangerous. When you are watching the waves, remember to do this from a safe distance so that there is no danger of your child being caught in the undertow, as the water recedes.

Patterns in the sand

As you walk along a sandy shore at low tide, notice the

ridges in the sand. Ask your child if he can tell you what has caused these. Discuss the effect of the waves on the sand as they roll in and out. Look out for sand pitted by recent rain storms and swirly patterns made by shells being spun round in the waves. Can your child tell you who or what has made the various footprints in the sand (humans, dogs and birds)? Point out sand that has been blown by the wind into huge sand dunes or tiny peaks. Show your child the coarse grass that often grows on dunes and the stones that often appear at the top of tiny peaks.

Activity – Let your child experiment by digging in both dry and wet sand in different areas of the beach. What happens when he tries to build a sandcastle with dry sand? Does it work when he builds the sandcastle with wet sand? The wet sand holds it shape whereas dry sand collapses. The waves are shaping the wet sand in the same way that he does when he builds sandcastles, whereas the wind blows the dry sand easily.

Pebbles

On most beaches, you will find a selection of pebbles. Notice how many of these have been rounded and made very smooth by the effect of the sea rolling them around. Point out how dull most pebbles look when they are dry and how beautiful when wet.

Activity – Ask your child to describe some dry pebbles on the beach. What colour are they and are they shiny or dull? Ask him to put the pebbles in a bucket full of water. What do they look like when he takes them out of the water? What has caused them to look so different? Can your child think of other things which look very different when they are wet or dry? (roof tiles, paving stones, kitchen floors).

Driftwood

You will often find driftwood on the beach. Notice how this has also been made very smooth by the action of the waves and is sometimes moulded into the most beautiful shapes. Do these shapes remind your child of anything in particular?

High-tide mark
If you walk along the high-tide mark, you will find lots of debris washed up there. Notice the sea-birds scavenging around, looking for food. Look out for different kinds of seaweed, shells, crab shells, sea urchins, cuttlefish and possibly other sea creatures (especially following storms). Sadly, you will all too often find plastic and glass rubbish as well, washed ashore from boats. Watch out for tar from spilt oil.

Activity – This is a good opportunity to remind your child about the necessity for taking rubbish home and disposing of it carefully, in order to avoid this kind of pollution. Emphasise the dangers of plastic, glass and oil to humans, birds and sea life.

SKIES

Aeroplane vapour trails
Encourage your child to look out for these trails in the sky. What does he think has caused them? Notice that they are only visible against a blue sky. Look out for the various different shapes of these vapour rails – some thin straight lines, directly behind aircraft, some wider trails, as they later spread out and others which are blown into beautiful shapes, resembling ferns, as the wind catches the trail. Notice how the blue sky is often cut dramatically in two by these white areas.

Activity – Encourage your child to use his imagination to tell you what shapes the aeroplanes have drawn in the sky – the more fantastic the better!

Cloud formations
Look out for different types of clouds on different days, indicating rainy (solid, grey skies), thundery (cauliflower-shaped, dark grey clouds), windy (whispy, white clouds) and

fine weather (fluffy, white, cotton-wool clouds). On occasions, separate clouds are visible, while at other times, the clouds merge into each other to give an overall sky colour.

Activity – Once you have shown your child the different shapes of cloud and explained what they mean, can he become a 'weather forecaster' and suggest what you and he should wear when you go out. Will it be hot/cold/wet/dry?

Sun's rays shining through the clouds
Point out this very beautiful phenomenon when you cannot see the sun but its rays shine down through the clouds. Can your child tell you where the rays are coming from?

Activity – Again, encourage use of his imagination by asking him to make up a story of what could be behind the cloud causing such a strange effect in the sky.

Rainbows
Look at all the different colours in the rainbow. Can he see them all – red, orange, yellow, green, blue, indigo and violet? Why is he seeing the rainbow now and not at other times? Explain how the effect is produced when there is rain and sunshine together.

Activity – Have fun painting a rainbow, or making one with small pieces of coloured paper, when you get home.

Sunsets
Notice how the sky turns the most beautiful shades of red, yellow and purple as the sun sinks down behind the clouds. As your child looks at the sunset, point out how everything in front of the bright sun looks black. Objects become 'silhouetted' against the bright red, pink and orange.

Activity – Let your child create his own sunsets by painting water onto drawing paper until it is quite wet and then putting on blobs of bright red, orange and purple paint, allowing the colours to mix freely. Another way to create the same effect is to glue torn strips of tissue paper, in appropriate colours, over each other in a random pattern. When the 'sunsets' are dry, add some silhouetted objects to the pictures, using thick black felt-tip pen, or by sticking on black paper shapes.

WOODLAND

Sun's rays shining down through the trees

Encourage your child to look at the lovely light effects observed in a wood when the sun is shining. What does he think causes these? Point out how the sun shines onto and through the leaves of the trees, thus producing dappled effects on the wood 'floor'.

Activity – Can your child see this effect elsewhere? Look out for plants causing similar dappled effects in the garden or park. At home, let him experiment by putting a colander between a light source and a piece of white paper on the floor. Notice the same effect. Again, the light is only coming through the holes in the colander, like the gaps in the trees.

Broken branches and twigs

Look out for interesting pieces of wood or bark. Pick them up and turn them around to see how they change.

Activity – Encourage your child's imagination by seeing if he can 'see' some of these pieces of wood as something else. Do any of them remind him of people, animals and so on? If he was able to break bits off would they suggest something more to him?

Big tree roots

Look out for roots protruding above the surface of the soil. These can be quite substantial. Explain the function of the tree's roots.

Activity – Can he follow the root system out from the tree?

Look out for large roots branching into smaller ones as they go further away from the tree.

Rotting wood
Let him feel how soft this gets in comparison to live wood. Show him how it is possible to remove strands of the rotting wood, whereas live wood is very solid.

Activity – Let your child explore the rotting tree trunks for minibeasts. How many different ones can he identify?

Markings on cut tree trunks
Look at the grain and markings on cut tree trunks and see how these form a circular pattern. Can your child tell you why there are several concentric rings in the cut tree trunk? Discuss the fact that this indicates the age of the tree.

Activity – Encourage your child to help you to count the circles. Explain that each circle shows one year's growth. How old is that tree?

Wood 'floor' debris
Point out the carpet of dead leaves and pine needles that often covers the 'floor' of a wood, especially in the autumn, as leaves fall.

Activity – Can your child explain why there is most of this debris in autumn? Explain that in spring and summer the leaves are on the trees, whereas in winter the leaves have often rotted away.

Wild flowers
Look out for all sorts of wild flowers. Tell your child the names of some of the common ones, for example, bluebells. Explain that he shouldn't pick these flowers. They should be left for everyone to enjoy.

Activity – When you get home, look at books of wild flowers. Did he see any of these in the wood?

GARDENS

Seasonal colours in the garden

Notice how the colours get brighter and more profuse in summer. In winter, gardens are very bare, with no colour on the trees. In spring, bright green leaves start to appear on the trees, together with flowering shrubs and flowers. In summer, leaves on the trees are fully opened in every shade of green and there is a mass of other colour around. Autumn sees leaves beginning to turn red and brown before they fall off, leaving the trees bare again.

Activity – Can your child tell you which season it is from looking at the garden? Let him paint or make a collage of a garden in the four different seasons.

Flowers

Encourage him to look very carefully at the flowers in your garden. Notice different petal shapes and the delicate markings and subtle variations of colour that often occur.

Activity – Make daisy chains together with your child and count how many petals there are on a daisy by gradually stripping them off one by one.

Spiders' webs

Look out for webs made much more visible by dew. Rain drops sit on the web and highlight the beautiful and intricate shape of it. Note how strong the web must be so that it is not destroyed by the weight of the water. In the winter, you may be lucky enough to find webs covered in frost, emphasising their shape in the same way.

Activity – See if your child can see the spider in the web or, indeed, any prey that is caught in it. Look carefully at the shapes involved. Can he draw a web with white chalk on black paper?

WEATHER

Rain

Look at the pavements and roads when it has been raining, especially once it is dark. Notice the wonderful glistening which occurs when the streetlights and car headlights shine down on the wet surface. When you are driving in the rain, in the dark, show your child how the car's headlights light up a very shiny road and highlight the spray from excess water on the road's surface.

Activity – Ask your child to look out for reflections on wet surfaces. When walking along the pavement when it has been raining, look out for the multicoloured effects you may be able to see in the gutter, caused by oil dispersing on water. Why might your child see these patterns at the side of the road? Explain how some oil escapes from cars when they are parked at the roadside. Can he tell you what will happen when the sun comes out again?

Sun

Point out what happens to pot plants or window boxes when it is very hot and sunny. Show him how the flowers droop over and dry up.

Look out for dark shadows when the sun is shining brightly.

Activity – Can your child tell you why flowers droop in the hot sun and what he needs to do about it to rectify the situation? Let him water the flowers and watch them stand up straight again. To show him that the flower stem has actually acted as a straw and sucked up the water, put a carnation in coloured water and watch as the flower head turns the same colour as the water.

Can your child identify what has caused which shadows? Have fun making puppet character shadows by moving your hands in front of a light source.

PATTERNS

Tiles

Tiles on house walls and garden walls are often slightly different colours and form beautiful, if somewhat irregular patterns. Can your child find any other patterns, for example, mosaic pathways or railings near his house?

Activity – Let your child make a pattern, suitable for a wall or path, by arranging playing cards, post-cards or books. Some of these patterns will be regular and some irregular. Try giving your child a defined space to use and see if he can fill it as fully as possible, by turning some of the units through 90 degrees.

Tyres and soles of shoes

Notice the patterns made by car tyres on muddy or wet roads. When we walk in mud or rain, our shoes leave the same sort of marks.

Activity – Let your child make paint patterns. Let him stand in some poster paint wearing old wellington boots and then walk over some thick white paper.

Ripples in still water

Point out the series of circles produced when stones are thrown into still water. The same effect is produced by ducks diving for weed. Notice how these circles get gradually bigger and bigger.

Activity – Let your child drop a marble into a wide bowl of water to see this effect.

SHAPES

Look out for specific shapes while out and about. For example:

- rectangles in brickwork and gates

- triangles in roofs
- circles in road signs
- squares in windows.

Activity – Using commercial shapes, or some you have cut out at home, encourage your child to produce a picture, using some of these shapes. He can add to the picture, as necessary, with his own drawings.

ROADS

Road markings and signs

Look out for different markings on the roads, such as lines in the middle of the road, different lines close to the pavement, speed traps, parking bays, speed limit restrictions, warnings to slow down, etc. What colours are used to paint these? Why does your child think those colours have been chosen? Point out the various road signs. Can he guess what any of these mean? Explain some of the easier ones, for example, school, STOP, cross roads, roundabout, etc.

Activity – Give your child some dark grey paper and several colours of poster paint, including yellow, white and red. Explain that this paper represents the road and your child is going to try and find which colour is the most suitable for making marks on the 'road', bearing in mind that it is very important for these markings to be seen. Encourage him to try out the various shades of paint, to see which colour is the most visible. Hopefully, he will understand why white, yellow and red are used.

Zebra crossings and pelican crossings

Look out for the bright orange beacon, marking a zebra crossing, together with the black and white stripes across the road. Explain that this is one of the safe places to cross the road, using the Green Cross Code. Explain the difference between a zebra crossing and a pelican crossing. A pelican crossing is located at traffic lights – there is no orange beacon or special marking on the road. When it is safe to cross, there will be a picture of a green, walking man on the traffic lights and when you must wait, there will be a stationary red man.

Activity – Use this as an opportunity to make sure your child knows what to do to cross the road safely and encourage him to tell you where you should cross. Practise crossing safely, making sure you hold his hand.

Streetlights
Notice how these are evenly spaced along motorways and main roads. When you drive along these roads, your child will be able to see a regular moving pattern, produced by the car moving past the streetlights. A very similar effect is produced when you drive past railings.

MOVEMENT
Squirrels
Watch these little creatures in your garden or the park and notice how they scamper about, almost turning somersaults as they fly around looking for food, tearing up, down and round and round trees.

Activity – Encourage your child to take lots of exercise by running around in the same way as these little animals.

Cats
Encourage your child to watch a cat hunting, from a safe distance. Notice how they creep along almost imperceptibly before finally pouncing on their prey.

Activity – Play a game like 'Grandmother's Footsteps' for fun and to encourage your child to move slowly and silently.

Birds

Watch these as they hop from branch to branch, or along
the ground, pecking at berries or at the ground for worms.
Notice how they are able to hang tightly onto branches
when the wind blows them around. Watch how different
birds eat their food. For instance, smashing snail shells to
get at the soft snail inside, cracking open sea shells to eat
the soft interior, pecking at nuts or pulling up worms.

Watch other birds, for example, seagulls or birds of prey,
swirling around high in the air as they get caught on the
thermal air streams. Notice how they simply glide around
with wings outstretched, but without any flapping of wings.
Compare this easy, graceful movement to gliders, which
move in much the same way.

Activity – Look at bird books with your child to notice the
different sizes of various birds and the different colouring of
male and female birds. Point out different beaks which vary
according to the type of food the birds eat.

Helicopters

Look out for these noisy machines, with their rotor blades
whizzing around on top of them. Watch them as they come
into land, hovering above the ground, before eventually
touching down.

Activity – Try to find some dragonflies to watch – you will
usually find them near ponds and pools of water. Notice the
similarities in their movement to that of helicopters. They
are often to be found hovering above the water. Explain that
though they both hover, dragonflies have wide wings instead
of rotor blades and their flight is silent.

KEYS

Give your child a selection of old keys to examine. Show
him how these vary infinitely, so that they can be used for
locking lots of different doors and cars. Notice the huge

variety of shapes and how even keys which look quite similar are different when you compare them closely.

BUTTONS

If you have a box full of buttons, use this as an observation and sorting exercise for your child. Let him explore the box and sort buttons according to his own criteria – size, colour, shape, number of holes and so on.

COINS

Give your child a pile of change, with all the coins in common use. How many different coins can he find? Encourage him to look carefully at them all and describe the size, colour and shape. Explain whose head is on the back of all the coins and point out the various designs on the front. Can your child see the numbers on the coins, corresponding to their value? Look for the dates, showing when the coins were minted.

Activity – Show your child how to make a rubbing of the designs on the coins. Use a small piece of Blu-tak to anchor the coin to the table and tape a piece of plain paper over the top. Now let your child rub over the coin with a wax crayon on its side and reproduce the coin design.

Opportunties for Learning

4

Learning in the Home

Always try to relate children's new learning to experiences
they have already had. This way, they are much more likely
to want to think about things and to be able to understand.
Time spent in the house in everyday activities can be very
productive to the learning process, if you take every
opportunity to point out what your child can learn from
what is going on around him.

BATHROOM

Most young children enjoy bathtime very much. It is a time
for them to relax and enjoy discoveries – to learn without
realising that they have. Bathrooms are full of interesting
things and, so long as care is taken, can provide an ideal
learning environment.

The washing sequence
Ask your child to consider what he has to do, in what order,
to have a bath and wash his hair. It may help him to
remember the sequence of everything if he thinks about
bathing his doll or toy. Before he does any of these things,
can he give you a complete list? Include getting undressed,
putting the plug in the bath, running both hot and cold
water into the bath, testing for the correct temperature,
getting in, washing his body with soap, washing his hair
with shampoo, rinsing, getting out and drying carefully with
a towel.

Different materials
Baths, basins and pipes can be metal, plastic or ceramic.

There are shiny mirrors, varnished cork tiles, metal towel rails etc. What different materials can your child identify in the bathroom? Point out the metal or plastic of the bath itself. How can he tell which it is? Allow your child to examine a collection of several examples of metal and plastic objects, for example, a new 2p or 10p coin and plastic money, stainless steel and plastic cutlery, toy cars in both metal and plastic. Encourage him to consider some of their properties such as temperature, appearance and sound when tapped gently. Before filling the bath, discuss the cold of the metal and the relative warmth of the plastic. Having made this investigation, can he tell you whether his bath is metal or plastic?

What are the pipes made of? If the pipes are not painted, notice the appearance of the pipes. Are they dull or shiny? Which does he think are metal and which are plastic? If the pipes are painted, how could he tell which are which? Wait for your child's own ideas and then talk about the different sounds the two materials might make when tapped gently with a coin. Warn him that pipes carrying hot water can get very hot and he should never touch them. However, to let him see which pipes are carrying hot water and which cold, you could let him touch your hands after you have touched the pipes, to tell which is which.

Look for shiny metal towel rails and mirrors. What happens to the mirror when hot water is run into the bath? Notice how it mists up. Let him write in the mist so that he can see that it is water which has collected on the cold mirror. Where has he seen this effect before? Remind him about misted up windows in the house and car when it is warm inside and cold outside. What is on the floor of the bathroom – shiny, slippery tiles or warm, soft carpet?

Taps and running and spraying water

Look specifically at taps. How does he know which is the hot and which is the cold? Point out H and C letters and emphasise the sounds of the letters. What does he think these might stand for? Some taps have red and blue dots. What do these mean? Can he think of other things which might give them a clue, for example, fires and hobs glowing red, grey/blue pictures in books depicting cold, wintry days. Look at the size of the taps. Why should bath taps be bigger than those on the basin? Ask him to think about the space that the water has to fill and therefore how quickly the water needs to come in. Give him a plastic jug with a wide lip, a metal teapot with a narrow spout and a plastic container so that he can experiment and discover that it is quicker to fill the container with the jug, rather than the teapot. Water will come out of the wide jug at a faster rate than the narrow teapot. This obviously applies to the taps as well.

Look at showers. Notice the holes in the shower head. Notice the effect this has on the water jet, compared to the jet which comes out of the tap. Let him stand under the shower and feel the fine spray. Let him play with a plastic jug and a colander in the bath, which will allow him to see at close quarters the differences of simply pouring water from a jug and pouring water through a set of small holes in the colander.

Pipes and drainage
Where does the water go when he takes the plug out of the bath? Look for the pipes and where they go. Ask where the pipes might go when they disappear into the wall. (Another time, show him the drains outside, with the pipes running into them.) Notice two pipes coming in for the two taps – hot and cold – and one going out for the waste.

Sounds
Running water and swirling water, as it drains away, make very distinctive noises. Listen to the noises water makes. Where else might he have heard noises like that? Consider the seaside and the noise of waves running up and down the shore. Think also of doing the washing-up and the noise dishwashers and washing machines make.

Friction
Many of the surfaces found in a bathroom will get very

slippery as they get wet. Slippery surfaces are very smooth and offer no resistance, unlike carpeted floors.

Why does he have to be careful when he gets into and out of the bath? Ask your child to run his hands over the surface of the bath and feel the smooth, slippery surface to remind him what plastic feels like when it is wet. Smooth, bare feet will slip on smooth, wet surfaces (the bath). Bathroom floors are often tiles, cork or lino, all of which are very smooth and become very slippery when wet.

BEDROOM

Children should feel comfortable in their own bedrooms. They are not just places for sleeping although this is obviously important. They should also be places where they can feel they have privacy and somewhere where they can keep all their possessions safely. Because they are multi-purpose rooms, they contain lots of interesting things.

Furniture

Help your child to realise why we need shelves of different shapes and sizes by encouraging him to consider the various books and other objects he might want to put on these. Are they all the same size and shape? Ask him to look at both the height and width of books. Some are tall and thin and need narrow shelves which are set wide apart, while others are short and wide, needing wide shelves set quite close together.

Discuss wardrobes and cupboards. Cupboards have shelves, whereas wardrobes have rails on which to hang clothes. Point out the position of the rails in your child's wardrobe. Why could you not hang your clothes in his wardrobe? Could he hang his clothes in yours? Discuss the sensible use of space.

Why might he have a desk or table in his room? Talk about the sort of activities he might wish to do, such as drawing, reading or building models and the need for somewhere to sit and do these activities.

Curtains and blinds

Look at the windows in his room. Why does he need to
have curtains or blinds on his windows? Talk about keeping
out the light. In summer, it gets light early in the morning
and stays light late into the evening. Without curtains or
blinds, the room would be full of light, making going to
sleep much harder and waking your child too early in the
morning. In winter, in contrast, it is dark much earlier and
children are often required to get up when it is still dark.
Curtains and blinds give the room a cosy feel and shut out
the dark which some children find frightening. Discuss
waking up. Adults and children use alarm clocks to wake
themselves up. How does the animal and bird life outside
wake up? Talk about a cock crowing.

Duvets, sheets and blankets

Bedding can consist of sheets and blankets or duvets. Sheets
cover the mattress and the child's body. Duvets and
blankets provide the warmth. Duvets are very light but trap
warm air from the body in the many feathers or fibres which
are inside them. Blankets are much heavier and several of
them provide a protective barrier for the body, stopping
warm air from escaping. Can your child think of other
things which work in this way? Remind him about his
padded coat which keeps him warm on very cold days. Let
him try to carry your thick winter coat to appreciate how
heavy it is.

Different textures of various soft furnishings

How many textures can your child identify? Extend his
vocabulary for describing these. Bedrooms are full of
exciting textures. Most children have a multitude of cuddly
toys – furry teddies, smooth, shiny seals, soft, manipulative
bean-bag toys. Duvets are light, thick and warm, bedcovers
can be rough or smooth, carpets and rugs are often lovely
to walk on in bare feet because they feel warm and cosy.
Large bean bags are very satisfying to sink into because they
take on the shape of your body. Blow-up arm chairs made
of plastic are bouncy and squeaky. Consider other words to

describe the various textures, for example, fluffy, velvety, sleek, comforting, rubbery and so on.

Lights, heaters, radios, tape recorders and other items in the bedroom

Ask your child to find all the things in his room which work using electricity. These could include the overhead light, a bedside light, a radio, a tape recorder, a heater, an electric clock etc. Show him how you have to plug these in to the electricity supply to make them work, at the same time warning him of the dangers associated with plugs, wires and electricity in general. Explain how the light switch makes the connection between the lights and the electricity supply. Talk about power cuts and explain what happens during one of these. Many appliances cease to work during power cuts, but some will continue to work, using a different power source, for example, batteries. Let him look at the innards of a torch, to see how the batteries fit in and how wires make connections with both the batteries and the bulb. Can he think of other toys he has which use batteries. Does his radio or tape recorder use batteries?

KITCHEN

Young children spend a great deal of time at home and, in reality, many families spend much of their time in the central room of any house – the kitchen. The kitchen is full of fascinating things and provides great opportunities for learning. However, when using the kitchen as a place of learning, safety must be your first consideration. Many things which happen in the kitchen can be related to things the children may have experienced elsewhere.

Safety

The kitchen provides the ideal place for instilling in your child some very important lessons about safety. Young children should never be left unsupervised in a kitchen. There are too many potential dangers. They need to know about the dangers of both gas and electricity. In some ways, a gas flame is easier to identify as an immediate danger, as children have usually been warned about fires and flames. (The unlit gas poses a different danger.) However, the intense heat produced by an electric hob may not be so easy to see, because some do not immediately glow red to warn the user to take care. Saucepans and utensils get hot as well as hobs and ovens and need to be handled with care. Most kitchens have floors which can easily be cleaned and therefore get slippery when wet. Your child needs to be warned about this too. When helping you to cook, he needs to understand that sharp knives, boiling water and steam are all dangerous.

Cookers and hobs

These come in all shapes and sizes now, sometimes free-standing, sometimes integrated, in a variety of colours. Before showing your child anything, remind him that touching anything in the kitchen without your permission is not allowed, because it can be very dangerous. There are many things to notice when looking at cookers, but one of the most interesting for your child is likely to be the pictures and lights on control panels and dials. Ask him to look out for such things as a **hand**, indicating manual control, a **clock** for timed cooking, a **bell** for the timer. Why are these symbols suitable ones to use? Let him listen to the timer buzzer or bell.

Show him the time display on the cooker and compare this with other clocks in your house. If you have a mixture of digital and analogue clocks in your house, make the connection between the two as simply as possible by concentrating solely on the hours for now. How will he know when the oven is on? Show him how the various dials light up the control panel when they are turned. Let him listen out for the purring noise when fan ovens are turned on. Emphasise again the safety aspects and impress on him that, although it is very interesting to look at the control panels and how they work, he must **never** fiddle with oven dials himself. He must always ask you to show him.

Heating

Kitchens are usually warm places. Can your child suggest why this should be? As well as radiators giving out heat, the room is heated when people are cooking, as both the hob and the oven provide heat when they are on.

Taps and sinks

In many kitchens, there is one mixer tap in the sink, rather than two separate ones for hot and cold water. Why does your child think this is? Explain that having one mixer tap allows you to have a stream of water at exactly the right temperature, by adjusting the flow of cold and hot water. When in the kitchen, you probably wash your hands more than at any other time and having warm, rather than hot or cold water is much more convenient.

Look at sink sizes and shapes. What are they made of – stainless steel or plastic? Many sinks have two compartments – one large and one small. Can your child suggest a reason for this, for example, soaking washing-up, cleaning vegetables or stacking dishes. Point out the draining board. What is this used for?

Cooking utensils

Look at all the different types of cooking utensils, avoiding sharp knives. Ask your child to sort the different utensils into various groups. They might sort them by:

- material (wood, metal or plastic)

- mixing utensils (wooden spoons and whisks)

- chopping utensils (garlic presses, graters, potato mashers)

- utensils for smoothing (palette knives, spreaders and spatulas)

- utensils for squeezing (juicers, icing bags)

- utensils for draining (colanders, sieves, slotted spoons)

- measuring utensils (spoons, jugs).

Discuss why the various utensils are made out of different materials.

Look at weighing scales – those that work like a see-saw, with weights, and those that show the weight on a dial. Why do we need to be able to weigh food?

Washing-up

Ask your child to help you wash up. Let him fill the sink with warm water and put in the washing-up liquid, creating bubbles by stirring it with his hand. Why do we use washing-up liquid? Why do we use warm water? If you have a dishwasher, let your child look inside it and see where all the plates, cups and cutlery are stacked so that they wash clean. Look for the arms which spin round, spraying water

...to avoid too many bubbles, a different kind of detergent is used.

over the contents of the machine when it is switched on. Do we use washing-up liquid in the machine? Can your child think why not? If he can create lots of bubbles by stirring gently with this hand, what does he think would happen when the arms of the machine spin round? To avoid too many bubbles, a different kind of detergent is used in the form of a tablet or powder.

Cooking

Let your child help you to make a cake. Ask him to say what you will need (aprons, bowl, spoons, cake tin, scales etc.) and what you must do, in what order. Look at recipe books and choose a recipe to find out the ingredients you will need. Follow your child's sequence, frequently asking him what you should do next, only correcting him if he is unable to see when he has the order wrong. How will he know when the cake is cooked?

Let him watch you whisk cream. Show him how the cream starts off as a runny liquid, gradually becoming thicker and thicker as you use the whisk. When the cream is nearly whisked, it will start to hold its shape, producing beautiful swirling patterns on the top. If you have any to spare, show him what happens when you continue to whisk beyond the crucial point.

Fridges, freezers and washing machines

Look at other appliances in the kitchen, including fridges, freezers and washing machines. Can your child tell you what these are used for? Both fridges and freezers keep things cold. What is the difference? Under careful supervision, let him touch food which has just been taken out of the fridge and food which has just come out of the freezer. Point out that freezer food is at a much lower temperature and is frozen hard, like ice cream, whereas refrigerated food is simply chilled, like a cold drink. Frozen food lasts much longer.

The washing machine washes clothes, rinses the soap off them and spins them dry, by spinning the tub round and round, just like his spinning top.

5

Learning While Shopping

All children go shopping with their parents and others who look after them. Different shop environments therefore provide the ideal opportunity for examining, discovering, reasoning and learning. The general idea is to show your child as much as possible and therefore to spark off an interest in their environment and a genuine desire to find out why things are the way they are.

Before you even get inside any shops, there will often be a number of interesting talking points. Many shopping malls have entry doors which work on a 'magic eye' system and open automatically as you go past them. Show your child where the 'eye', which detects something passing, is likely to be. Explain that this triggers a mechanism for opening the doors. When you go into large department stores, a number of them will have revolving doors as well as conventional ones. Show your child how these doors turn round as you push them and how they have compartments for several people to enter the shop together. Help your child to enter and leave these doors safely, by watching carefully to find out when he needs to move quickly in or out.

You will come across escalators in some of the malls and bigger shops. Let your child watch people going up and down on these. Are they climbing the staircase? Explain that they are actually standing still whereas the staircase itself is moving. When he has watched for a while and worked out what is going on, help him to get on and off the escalator safely. Make sure that he realises that he should continue to walk slowly forward as he steps off the escalator.

SUPERMARKET

Supermarkets provide many of the family's general needs and many different items can be bought there. However, most shopping trips to such shops will involve buying food, hence the major concentration on this area of the shop.

Trolleys and baskets

As you go into the supermarket, notice the different types of basket and trolleys. There are usually at least three different ones – big trolleys for weekly shops, smaller ones for small amounts of food and baskets for carrying a few items. Some are attached to other trolleys and can only be released by feeding in money. Allow your child to help you put in the money to release the trolley and to collect the money again when you return the trolley. Most trolleys have child seats built into them. Why does your child think this is? Notice straps fitted to some for keeping active toddlers in place!

Positioning of food in different areas of the supermarket

All supermarkets group different types of food in different areas of the shop. Their layout is not necessarily the same as other supermarkets, but there will be logic behind it. Before going shopping, involve your child in looking through kitchen cupboards to find out what you need and encourage him to help you make a list, sorting the food on your list into various categories. Can he suggest simple categories to you, for example, drinks, fruit, vegetables, baby food, freezer food, bread and cakes, meat and fish, fridge food (milk, yoghurt, cheese etc.)? Take this list to the supermarket and encourage your child to suggest to you where you might find some of the simpler items you have on your list. For instance, the apples are here, can you find the bananas for me? The milk is here, so where might I find the yoghurt? The frozen food is in a freezer, so where will I find the ice cream?

...so where might I find the yoghurt?

Tins of food

As you go round the area where tinned food is stacked, encourage your child to look at the various tins on display. Can he tell you what will be inside these tins? Does he need to be able to read the label or can he tell you what will be inside simply by looking at the outside? What about jars and packets? Note that jars do not need pictures in the same way as tins, because you can see through them. Some packets have pictures on them, some have transparent windows so that you can see the contents inside the packages, while others only have writing.

Types of packaging

Food and drink comes in all shapes and sizes. Packaging has to suit the items it is for. Consider different kinds of packaging and think about why certain types are used for certain types of food. What is the purpose of the packaging? Is it to keep food fresh, to make it look attractive or to keep several items of food together? In practice, it will usually be a mixture of all these things.

Liquids need to be in waterproof packaging such as glass (used less and less), tin, plastic, foil or waxed cardboard. Can your child find examples of all these in the supermarket? Encourage him to look at the shelves of soft drinks for examples of all these. Drinks are not the only items that need waterproof wrapping. Many foods also 'leak'. Consider meat, fish and poultry, ready-made meals, yoghurts, bacon, cheese and so on. Why can't these products be wrapped in ordinary paper? Look at what sort of packaging these products have and notice that many are wrapped in cling film, plastic containers or bags.

What types of food can be wrapped in paper and cardboard? Look for packets of biscuits, cereals, flour, egg boxes etc. and note that all these contain dry foods. Develop this discussion by asking your child what he thinks we should do with the packaging when we have finished with it. Talk about which of the materials can be recycled and why recycling is a good idea. If possible, take your child to a recycling centre and let him see what happens for himself.

Bar codes

Show your child what a bar code looks like and encourage him to find these on a variety of goods which you have bought. All goods will have one on their packaging somewhere and a special machine at the checkout will read the lines to tell the sales assistants how much to charge for the goods. Explain that this makes it much quicker and easier at the checkout.

The sounds various foods make

If tins, packets and jars do not have pictures on them, how else can you tell what is inside them? Consider the sounds foods and drinks make inside their packaging. Without encouraging children to shake everything in sight, let them listen to a variety of foods. They will notice that liquids make a sloshing sound, rice, dry pasta and cereals rattle. Some fruits and vegetables make squeaking noises inside their packaging.

Different smells in different areas of the supermarket

Different areas of the supermarket will smell different. Point out the lovely fresh smells of fruit in the fresh produce area, the fragrant smells of soap and shampoo in the chemist section, the smell of freshly baked bread and rolls in the bakery, the scent of flowers in the garden area and the smells of soap powder and cleaning agents in the household section. Ask him to close his eyes and tell you when you reach certain areas of the supermarket, just by using his sense of smell.

Meat, fish and delicatessen counters

Within the supermarket, there are often separate counters for fresh fish, raw meat and a delicatessen which has a selection of cold meats, cheeses and pâtés etc. At the delicatessen counter, items are weighed out carefully – look out for the scales – and packed in polythene bags. Point out the meat slicer, which can produce very thin slices of meat. Remind your child that these slicers are extremely sharp and can be dangerous. Fresh meat often needs to be cut to size, requiring very sharp knives and sometimes, special saws, to cut through bones. Watch as the butcher skilfully does this.

Look out for the enormous variety of fresh fish available. Explain that shellfish is fish that has a hard shell, for example, prawns, mussels and crabs. Point out the differences in size and shape of all these fish. Notice the beautiful colouring on some of them and how ugly others can look. Explain how prawns and lobsters are a bluish colour when they are raw, but turn pink once they are cooked. Is your shop selling raw or cooked shellfish, or both?

Fresh bakery counter

There are often in-store bakeries in supermarkets. Look out for these. Can your child smell the freshly baked bread? If you pick up a loaf, it may still be warm. Let your child feel this. Can he tell you why this is? Look out for the enormous variety of different breads available, both brown and white, in all shapes and sizes. Some bread comes already sliced. Look out for the slicing machines, which cut through whole loaves, turning them into thick or thin slices. If you have an egg slicer, which works in the same way, help him to slice a hard boiled egg when you get home.

Checkouts

When you reach the checkout, point out the different
checkout lanes, some of which are fast lanes for people with
only a very few items of shopping. Let your child help to
load the food onto the conveyor belt. Let him watch how
the belt moves the food towards the assistants as they
remove goods from the other end of it. They then scan them
and put them onto another conveyor belt at the other end of
the checkout. Watch how the second belt sends the goods to
the end of the checkout ready for you to pack them into the
plastic bags which are provided. Listen to the bleep of the
scanner as it scans bar codes and gives a readout of prices.
Show your child the visual display and let him see the
writing and figures that come up on it, telling you how
much you need to pay for each item of your shopping.

Car parks

Many supermarkets have a car park attached to them. They
may be single, multi-storey, inside or out in the open, under
ground or above. If you are in a multi-storey, point out the
narrow ramps as you go up or down to other floors. Ask
your child to look out for a space. When you have found
somewhere to park, how do you remember where you have
left the car? Show him the different numbers and letters in
each part of the car park, to help you. Cars go down or up
to road level by ramps, whereas pedestrians use lifts or
stairs. Tickets are often issued as you enter the car park and
you pay before leaving. Let your child come to the pay
station with you. Can he feed in the ticket and the correct
money? When you leave, approach the barrier slowly and
show your child how it lifts up when you feed in the paid
ticket.

Recycling banks

Bins for recycling glass, cans and paper are often located in
supermarket car parks. Let your child watch as you feed
bottles, cans and papers into the appropriate bins. Explain
what happens to these and why it is important to recycle
waste. If the bins are fairly accessible, you could let him feed

in the paper. (Glass is too easily broken and can banks often have wasps hanging around them.)

DEPARTMENT STORE CLOTHES SHOP

Seasonal differences in clothing

Note the different types of clothes in the shops when you go shopping at different times of year. In winter, there will be jerseys, thick coats and woollen dresses. In summer, you will find thin cotton dresses, T-shirts, swimming costumes and lightweight jackets. Discuss the properties of different materials. Let your child try on clothes made from various materials in order to test these properties. Why are certain materials used at certain times of year?

Different areas for different types of clothing

In big stores, how do we know where to find the different clothes we might wish to buy? Show your child where to find the store guide, with its alphabetical list. Discuss how the different categories of clothes might be described, for example, by type of clothing:

- dresses
- jumpers
- outdoor

by who the clothing is for

- women
- men
- children and babies

by the occasion the clothing is intended for

- daywear
- partywear
- sportswear.

Changing rooms and mirrors

Look out for changing rooms in the various areas of the store. Why do we need them? What will they have in them? To keep him occupied while you are trying on garments, ask your child to name everything he can find in the changing rooms. Point out large mirrors, sometimes two, so that you can see both your front and rear views (let him try this out), hooks on the walls and doors for hanging up clothes, perhaps a chair, bright lights, thin scarves for putting over your head to keep makeup from marking clothing. Let him look at the tag you are given when you enter the changing room. Sometimes this will have a number on it which corresponds to the number of garments you are taking in with you. Why do sales assistants need to know that? Explain the need for keeping a track of everything and making sure that nothing gets lost. Note different types of hangers for different clothes. Some also have clips to keep garments in place.

Payment desks and security tags

When you have chosen the clothes you want to buy, show your child both the price tag and the security tag attached to the clothes. Explain that security tags have to be removed from clothes before you leave the shop because otherwise alarms would be set off as you passed special points in the doorway. When you come to the pay desk, note how tickets on clothes are scanned in the same way as for food, with prices coming up on a visual display. Note also how the assistants remove the security tags with a special tool. Can your child tell you why these tags are put onto clothes?

CHILDREN'S TOY AND BOOK SHOP

Layout – different ages, toy type

Toys are likely to be grouped according to the type of toy or the age group the toy is intended for. See if your child can understand the links between toys which are grouped together in your toy shop.

Toys for different ages and types of play

Most children have a variety of toys that encourage different skills. Toys are designed with many objectives in mind. Some encourage imaginary play, some help children to be creative, some are for outdoor play and some are for comfort.

Activities

1. Ask your child to think about his own toys. Can he suggest similar alternatives for some of the toys he has. For example, if he has:
   - Lego bricks, what could he have instead, to build things with? (wooden blocks, other construction kits)
   - pencil crayons, what could he have instead, to draw with? (felt-tip pens, paints)
   - a tricycle, what else could he have to play with outside? (climbing frame, football)
   - a teddy bear (other soft toys)
   - model cars, what else could he play imaginary games with? (farm animals, play people).

2. What toys are suitable for babies and very young children? Can your child suggest a few?

3. Look at the book section in your toy shop. What type of books attract your child? Can he tell you why? Can he select a suitable book for his elder sibling or a friend's baby?

Play areas

If your toy shop has areas for play and toys which can be played with, why do the children think this might be? Discuss this in terms of keeping children occupied while parents are shopping, encouraging children and parents to buy similar toys and encouraging children and their parents back to the shop on other occasions.

SHOE SHOP
Different sizes for children, men, women
Explain that there are shoe sizes ranging from 1–12 for both children and adults – the smaller number in each category being the smaller shoe. Some shoes also come in different widths, ranging from A–E. The size and width of the shoe will be printed inside the shoe. Can your child find his size?

Different types of shoe
As in clothes shops, different areas of the shop will be dedicated to shoes for different people. There are many different types of shoe, designed for all sorts of purposes. Ask your child to tell you some of the shoes he has. His list might include boots, slippers, trainers and, depending whether it is summer or winter, sandals or more substantial walking shoes. Most shoes come packed in sturdy boxes. How does the assistant know which shoes are in which box? Tell him that all the boxes have pictures of the shoes stuck onto the end of them and the size is also printed on the end of the box. Let him look at the various boxes when you are trying on shoes, so that he can see this. Discuss the purposes of the various types of footwear. Why do children need more than one pair? Think about being both outside in various weather conditions and inside at various times of day.

Foot size gauge
The first thing the assistant does when you go to buy a new pair of shoes is to measure your foot. He does this with a special kind of ruler. Your foot sits comfortably into this, with your heel resting against one end. By bringing down a bar at the end of your foot, the assistant can read off the shoe size required. In order to get the correct width measurement, he tightens a special measuring tape around the ball of your foot, to take this reading. This special measuring ruler for feet is called a foot gauge. Why does the assistant need to measure your foot accurately?

Shoe horns

Next, you need to try on the shoes. Show your child the moulded shape and smoothness of a shoe horn and see if he can suggest to you how he might use it to help him to try on shoes without damaging them. When inserted into the back of the shoe, the shoe horn allows the foot to slide easily into the shoe.

Mirrors

Notice mirrors at ground level. Ask your child to explain to you why these might be at this height and not higher up on the wall.

Accessories – bags, tights, socks, polishes

Look at what the shoe shop is selling besides shoes. There might be handbags, tights, socks, polishes and shoe trees. Why do shoes need to be looked after? Why do they need to be polished? What purpose do shoe trees fulfil? At home, let your child see how trees stretch the leather, thus helping to prevent wrinkles from forming. Why do shoe shops sell handbags as well? Point out matching colours and designs.

CHEMIST

Can your child tell you when we would go to the chemist? Discuss looking after ourselves properly and getting better when we hurt ourselves or are feeling ill.

Dental items

What does your child need to look after his teeth properly? Discuss toothpaste and toothbrushes. Show your child the wide range of toothbrushes. Are any specifically designed for children? How does he know? Show him one with a big head. Why would such a toothbrush not be suitable for children?

Bath items

What does your child need in order to have a bath? Talk

about sponges and flannels, soap, perhaps bath oil or bubble bath and a bath cap, possibly a non-slip mat. You are likely to find all these items grouped together in one part of the chemist.

Hair items
Consider hairwashing. You will need shampoo and possibly conditioner, a hairbrush and comb, possibly hairbands and grips. Again, notice the huge choice of shampoos available. Do any particular ones attract your child? Can he tell you why?

First aid
What happens when your child hurts himself? If he has a cut knee, you are likely to put on a plaster. If he has a sore patch of skin, you are likely to put on some cream. Explain that these items are called first aid and can all be bought at the chemist. Chemists also sell first aid boxes containing many of the items that are required when people have minor accidents. Show him the shelves containing these items.

Prescriptions
What happens if your child is ill? When you take him to the doctor, the doctor will sometimes prescribe antibiotics. These cannot be bought over the counter, but need to be handed out at a special counter in the chemist. Show him all the special medicines that are stored behind this counter which can only be given out by the pharmacist. You have to take the doctor's written prescription to the counter where they will ask you to wait while the pharmacist finds the medicine and measures out how much you need. Tell him how important it is that you receive the correct medicine and know how much to take. The pharmacist sticks a label with your name and all these details onto all bottles and packets of medicines he prescribes. Let your child look at this when you receive the medicine.

FLORIST

Variety of flowers

As you go into the florist, notice first the overpowering scent of the huge variety of flowers. According to the time of year, there will obviously be different flowers in the shop. Notice differences in colour, size, shape and also all the different kinds of greenery available for flower arrangers. Can your child name any of the more well-known flowers such as roses, tulips, daffodils? Depending on his knowledge, add a few more, testing his ability to remember whenever you come across those flowers again.

Bouquets and floral arrangements

All florists have a bouquet and basket arranging service. Many sell these already made-up. Notice how bouquets and baskets are often made from flowers of similar or coordinating colours. Florists often finish their arrangements with coloured ribbon to match the arrangement. Point out the selection of coloured ribbon to your child. Which colour would he choose?

Real and artificial flowers

Many florists also sell artificial flowers. Show your child which is which. Does he think they look the same. Point out that artificial flowers are not growing, do not need water and will not die.

Activity – What are the major differences between real and artificial flowers? If you have some at home (a bit risky in the shop!), let your child feel and smell some of them. There will, of course, be no smell and the flowers themselves will feel completely different, although they may look remarkably real.

VIDEO SHOP

Children's video section

All video shops will have a section dedicated to videos for

children. How does your child choose the one he would like to see? Explain how the picture on the video box shows the child what the film is about. There will also be a title on the front. These boxes do not have the video inside, but are out on the shelf so that the customer can choose the video he wants.

Pay desk
When you have chosen the video you want, you must take the empty box to the pay desk where you must give it to the assistant, together with some money, in return for the film, in a plain box. Many videos have to be returned the following day, but some can be borrowed for longer, if the customer pays more. Can your child think of somewhere else where he can borrow things? Compare the process to that in a library. Point out that borrowing books is free, as long as you return them on time.

CARD SHOP

Different types of card
When you go to the shop to buy a card, ask your child to think about who the card is for and for what occasion. Show him how the cards are laid out in the shop in different areas, depending on what and who they are for. Look out for cards suitable for children, those for special age birthdays, with numbers on them, baby congratulation cards, Mother's and Father's Days cards.

Activity – Let your child help you to choose suitable cards for different members of the family and for special occasions. What would they like and what would be suitable? Help him to think about the recipient.

Special products for special birthdays
Look out for balloons and banners saying 'Happy Birthday', individual birthday cakes, birthday cake decorations and candles – including number candles, silver keys – for 21st birthdays, mugs and cuddly toys.

STREET MARKET

Different stalls

Markets often have lots of different stalls – fruit and vegetables and other foods, clothing, books, toys, handicrafts and so on. Explain that markets are like a number of small shops all on one site, out in the open.

Awnings

Because they are outside, each stall needs to have an awning over it in case it rains. The awning is also useful when it is very hot, to provide some shade.

GARDEN CENTRE

Different plants, shrubs and trees

Show your child the wide range of plants on sale, by wandering around the garden centre. Explain that these will change according to the time of year, as different plants flower at different times.

Hanging baskets and pot plants

To make it easy for people, garden centres also sell some flowers and plants already planted in pots or hanging baskets. Has your child seen these used as window boxes or hanging by front doors?

Bulbs and seeds

Many plants are grown from seeds or bulbs and garden centres always have a wide selection of these on sale. Show your child the picture on the packaging which tells him what the seeds or bulbs will grow into.

Compost and gravel

It is possible to buy large bags of compost and gravel for use in the garden. Point out that plants need good soil in order to grow well. Compost is like special food which can be added to soil to make the plants grow better. Gravel is often used on paths in gardens.

Paving stones

Show your child the large selection of paving stones on sale. Notice that they are available in all shapes and sizes. Where does he think these stones might be used? Explain that many gardens have an area which is often used as a patio and these stones are used for that. They are also used for paths. If some of the stones are used in a display, point out the patterns they can make.

Terracotta and stone pots and statues

Many plants are grown in pots and there will always be a wide selection of these for sale, ranging from quite small ones to enormous ones, in all shapes and sizes and sometimes, many colours. Many people like to have statues in their gardens and garden centres usually sell some of these. Encourage your child to say what he likes and dislikes in this respect.

Garden tools and supplies

In order to look after a garden properly, many tools and other equipment is needed. Can your child tell you what he would need to dig the garden? Talk about spades, forks and trowels. What might he need to tie up a plant which has fallen down? What does he need to water the flowers?

Garden furniture

In summer, people like to sit out and maybe eat in their gardens. Look out for tables and chairs and also parasols, which provide some shade. Point out the different materials used – wood, plastic and metal. What patterns and colours does your child like best?

6

Learning During Hospital, Doctor and Dentist Visits

HOSPITAL

Bearing in mind that some children can be rather upset about the prospect of being in hospital, the following ideas could provide welcome distractions for your child.

Wards

What does your child notice in his ward? Is it just for children? How can he tell? How are the beds arranged in the ward? How many children in his ward? Are there any cots for younger children? Is there anything to entertain them, such as television or games and toys?

Lifts

Notice how big the lifts are. Why does your child think this is? Link your discussion to the wheels on beds. The beds have wheels because they need to be moved around – not only around the ward, but also from one department of the hospital to another. How does your child think the hospital staff do this? Explain that the lifts have to be large enough for beds, as well as people, to fit in them.

Beds on wheels

How does his hospital bed differ from his bed at home? Consider wheels, brakes, height adjusters, side bars, bed heads and charts at the bottom of the bed. What is this bed made from? What is his bed at home made from?

Curtains on rails around beds

On the ceiling, between beds, is a curtain rail, to allow

curtains to be drawn around each bed. Why does your child think this is? Explain the need for privacy when children are being examined or washed.

Emergency buttons

Within easy reach of each bed is a red emergency button. Explain that this button should only be pressed if there is an immediate need for the doctor to come. Can your child tell you why the button is coloured red?

Identification tags

Explain that there are a lot of different patients in the hospital and doctors and nurses need to know exactly who they are seeing and what medicine or treatment they should be having. As patients are sometimes asleep and cannot be asked who they are, all patients have identification tags fitted to their wrists to avoid any confusion. Can your child tell you what is written on his tag?

Drips

Many patients on the ward will be fitted with drips. Gently discuss conditions which make it difficult for children to take food in the normal way, and explain the need sometimes, to deliver a constant supply of medicines. Drips can give food or medicine to the patient in an easy, constant and measured way. Notice the plastic bags which contain the food or medicine. This flows along tubes which are attached to the drip, inserted into the patient's hand. For many patients, these drips will be fitted to portable trolleys so that they can walk around with them.

X-ray machines

Talk about X-ray machines. Discuss the kinds of picture which these give you. Explain that X-rays allow the doctor to see what is going on inside the body, so he knows how to make it better. If possible, let your child examine an X-ray picture.

Nurses' and doctors' uniforms

Discuss the uniforms that both nurses, doctors and theatre staff wear. Why do people wear uniform? Discuss such things as:

- identification
- cleanliness
- practicality.

Stethoscopes

What are stethoscopes used for? Your child will probably have experienced his chest being listened to. Does he know what the doctor is listening to and what his heart should sound like? If possible, ask the doctor to explain and let him listen.

DOCTOR OR NURSE

Surgery reception

All surgeries have a reception desk. Talk your child through what you have to do when you arrive at the surgery for an appointment. Let him see the check-in process as you give your name and the receptionist goes through the appointment book or checks your name against a computer list. Some surgeries have a system of numbered cards to tell you when it is your turn, while others will individually call patients. If yours uses a system of numbered cards, let your child look at the numbers to see when it will be your turn. Can he tell you how many people are going to go in before you? What else is in the waiting room? Notice magazines, leaflets and toys. Why are they there?

Consulting rooms

When you reach the doctor's consulting room, ask your child to look out for

- a sink
- a bed

- weighing scales and a height measure
- a computer
- medical books and magazines.

Why does he think all these are needed by the doctor? Talk about the need to have clean hands when doctors are examining patients, the need for some patients to be lying down as the doctor examines them, the need to weigh and measure some patients, the need to look up notes about individual patients, which are stored in the computer and the need to look up information about various medicines in books.

Examination instruments
The doctor will have several instruments in his room. These will include stethoscopes, blood pressure monitors, throat swabs, eye and ear lights. Does your child know what all these do?

Discussing symptoms
If you are taking your child to the doctor, not yourself, encourage him to describe his own symptoms to the doctor, prompting him as necessary. It is a good idea to have discussed his symptoms a little before the visit to the doctor, suggesting what might possibly be wrong and why you think he needs to go to the doctor. Your child will probably have the opportunity to see some of the instruments he has been looking at being used, depending on his symptoms.

Prescriptions
If your child needs one, the doctor will write a prescription for him. Again, this may be an opportunity for your child to state his name or address, as the doctor writes the prescription. If the surgery is fully computerised, he will be able to watch the doctor type in details and the prescription being printed out. Does your child know what you have to do with this piece of paper?

Injections

Visits to the nurse, rather than the doctor might be for injections against various diseases. Encouraging your child to think about how things work can help to take his mind off the whole process if he is somewhat nervous. If possible, let him play with a syringe, without a needle, before the visit. This will allow him to see how liquid is taken up into the barrel of the syringe and how it is then expelled by pressing down on the plunger. Explain that the body only needs a very small amount of medicine injected into it in order for the person to develop immunity to the disease. To distract him, you could explain how the beating of the heart and its pumping of blood around the body is rather like the action of a syringe pushing liquid along a tube.

Routine weighing and measuring

Sometimes your child will visit the nurse to discover how much he weighs or measures. Show him the dials and measurements on the scales and the height measure. Can he remember how heavy and tall he is? Keep a record at home for comparison to let him see how he is growing.

DENTIST

Many adults have a fear of dentists, which is easy to pass on to children. To avoid this, explaining gently what he can expect to see and what will happen can be very helpful. At the same time, you will be increasing his understanding.

Reception area

Point out the receptionist in the entrance who will be sitting behind a desk. Can your child tell you some of the things on her desk? Look out for telephones, a computer, appointment books, calendars, pens and pencils. Can your child tell you why she needs all these things? Explain that as you come in, you have to check in at the reception desk so that the dentist knows that you have arrived for your appointment. The receptionist needs to have a record of everybody's appointments with all the different dentists, so that she knows who to expect and at what time. These will be recorded either on the computer or in the appointment book.

Waiting room

Ask your child to describe the waiting room to you. Look out for magazines for patients to read as they wait. What is available for children? Are there any books or toys for them to play with? How many chairs are there? Can he see any pictures on the walls, or other things to look at?

Are there any books or toys for them to play with?

Consulting room

This is the room where the dentist and her dental nurse actually work, mending people's teeth. Point out all the interesting things in it.

Adjustable dentist's chair

Hopefully, your dentist will be receptive to the idea of your child having a ride up and down in the dentist's chair. Explain that this chair is rather more like a bed than a chair. Let him see how the dentist pumps it up and down with his foot and how the head end of the chair can be lowered gradually to an almost flat position. Why does your child think this is necessary? Explain that mending teeth is a very precise job and that it is necessary for your dentist to be able to see very clearly what he is doing. Also, dentists have to see patients of many different sizes – both adults and children – and they therefore need adjustable equipment.

Adjustable light

The dentist needs a very bright light, to help him to see well. This light is attached to the ceiling above the chair, so that it shines down onto the patient's mouth. The light has handles on it so that the dentist can move it around easily, to get it into the correct position.

Drills and instruments

The dentist's instruments are all on an adjustable tray, within easy reach as he works. He will often sit on an adjustable, swivel chair. Ask the dentist to show your child the 'mirror on a stick' which helps him to see behind your child's teeth.

If your child is not just having his teeth checked, but is also to have a filling, explain why this is sometimes necessary, without frightening your child or causing him to feel guilty. Holes arise because food sometimes gets stuck alongside teeth and this food can cause teeth to decay. It is necessary to mend decayed teeth, because otherwise they would eventually fall out and make it difficult to chew food. Before holes in the teeth can be filled, this decay needs to be removed. This is when the dentist uses his drill. Explain that the special drill the dentist uses is much smaller than the one he might have seen you use at home. This drill emits a very high-pitched squeaking noise and will spray out water at the same time, to keep it cool.

The dentist's nurse uses a special sucking instrument, which works rather like a vacuum cleaner, to collect water from your child's mouth. This also makes a strange noise, which is nothing to worry about. Once the hole is clean, the dentist can use other instruments to push a filling into the hole in the tooth. Sometimes he uses another tool which puffs air at the tooth to dry it. Compare this to air dryers for drying hands. The dentist needs to make sure that these instruments are thoroughly cleaned after each use, so he uses a small microwave, like the one your child may have seen you use at home, to do this.

Water fountain
Beside the dentist's chair there is a small basin, together with a glass of coloured water. Explain that the water is coloured because it has got a special antiseptic pill dissolved in it. When the dentist is working on your child's teeth, your child will be asked to rinse his mouth out from time to time with this special water to keep it clean. He can spit into the basin, just like he does at home when he is cleaning his teeth with his own toothbrush. There are paper hankies beside the basin so that he can wipe his mouth afterwards.

Photographic covers for ceiling lights
To help patients feel relaxed, many dentist's surgeries have special photographic covers put over their bright ceiling lights. These are above the patients' head and provide a welcome visual distraction when the patient is feeling nervous. Equally, many surgeries play music for patients to listen to and there may well be other pictures around the walls to look at.

Dentist, dental nurse and hygienist
Most dentists work with a dental nurse. Both wear masks over their noses and mouths so that they do not either spread germs to their patients or catch them from them. Overalls or uniforms of some kind protect their clothes. Sometimes they wear special magnifying glasses so they can see very clearly. These can look rather odd, but are nothing to worry about. They also wear disposable rubber gloves, to make sure their hands are really clean.

The assistant will help the dentist by passing her things as she is mending the tooth. Can your child tell you why she puts a plastic cape around his neck before the dentist starts to work on his tooth?

The hygienist looks after teeth in a rather different way. She will not mend teeth, but helps them to keep healthy by cleaning them very well with a special brush attached to a machine. How can your child help to keep his teeth clean and healthy?

X-ray machines

Finally, point out the X-ray machines. Your child may well have had an X-ray in hospital, following a fall, in order to assess whether he has broken a limb and it is possible to get similar pictures of the inside of teeth. Can your child suggest why this might be necessary? Linking to his possible experience in hospital, point out that if there is unexplained pain in the mouth, an X-ray will often be able to show what is wrong. The machine can swivel round and is able to take pictures through the skin on the side of the face.

7

Learning While on Holiday

PARK OR GARDEN

Shapes

Look out for shapes in this natural environment. Point out the overall circular shape of many flower heads. Can your child see the two sizes of circles in many of these flowers? What shape are most petals making up flowers? Do they have straight or curved edges? When he has carefully looked at several flowers, (always remembering not to touch any which are poisonous), get him to examine leaf shapes. Point out the enormous variety of shape here. Show him how some leaves are single, whereas others are grouped together on a single stem. Some leaves are long and thin and even appear to have straight edges, whereas flowers, because they are made up of several petals, almost always appear rounded.

Activity – Using cut-out, adhesive shapes, encourage your child to make a shape picture of a garden, using the correct sort of shapes for the flowers and leaves.

Colours

Next, consider colours. Ask your child which colours he sees most often outside in the garden or park. Obviously, there is a preponderance of blue and green, but encourage him to look more carefully to discover different shades of the same colour. The colours he notices most will vary according to the time of year – yellow being a spring colour and rusty browns and reds being more visible in autumn. Is there any colour he never sees in the garden or park?

Activity – To test this out, get hold of a comprehensive paint colour chart and ask him to show you colours he has never seen outside, in the natural environment. If you can prove him wrong, so much the better (as along as you contradict him gently!)

Smells

Introducing your child to the delight of smells found in the park or garden is very important to develop his sense of smell. Encourage him to tell you which smells he likes and which he doesn't, together with his reasons, if possible. Try to include some unpleasant smells as well so he can really appreciate the difference. Examples of pleasant smells – roses (take care with the thorns!), lavender, lilac, stocks, honeysuckle; unpleasant smells include may, cat mint and Michaelmas daisies.

Activity – Can he identify his all-time favourite smell in the garden?

Girth of trees

Notice the enormous variety of trees. Can he tell you the difference between a bush and a tree? Point out that all trees have a single trunk coming out of the ground, which then supports the leaves at the top. Trees can be very small or immensely tall. Ask him to look carefully at the trunk of the tree. Can he see round it or is it too wide for him to be able to do this? Explain that the diameter or girth of the tree trunk is a very good indication as to the age of the tree, when comparing the same type of tree.

Activity – Play hide and seek, noting that the best hiding places are behind trees with big trunks.

Touch

Bark on trees varies enormously. Some trees have smooth bark, others are rough and still others have hairy trunks. Equally flowers and leaves can vary tremendously in texture – some being sticky, some soft, some prickly and some furry.

Activity – Play a guessing game with your child to see whether he can predict what a particular bark, flower or leaf will feel like. When he has guessed, let him test the accuracy of his guess by touching them. Wash hands carefully afterwards.

Finding cones, seeds and fruit

Look out for different seeds and cones growing on the trees. There are lots of different cones found on fir trees of different types. Many trees have very distinct seeds and fruit, for example, acorns, ash keys, sycamore keys, apples, cherries and conkers. Avoid berries, many of which are poisonous.

Activity – Let your child collect and open up ripe conkers and enjoy picking out the shiny, brown fruit. Can he identify the straight and the curved edges?

Alive or dead

Point out the difference between dead and alive plants and trees. Find and compare green leaves and dried-up brown ones.

Activity – Encourage your child to feel both a 'green stick' and a dry twig. Let him attempt to break each one by bending it. What happens? If he can't break it in his hand, invite him to step on it and look at the results. To reinforce the point, cut a dry twig and a green one with secateurs and show him the cut end. Point out that the live one is green or yellowy-white while the dead one is brown. Also, the dead twig will be totally dry, while the live one is wet. Can your child suggest why this is?

Effect of the wind

Notice how blossom is blown off the trees by strong winds and in autumn, leaves will be stripped from trees. In very strong winds, branches can be torn from trees.

Activity – Take your child out in the country after a gale and notice all the debris around the country lanes and roads.

Effect of rain

Look at the flowers in the garden after a heavy rainstorm. The flowers will have been flattened and many destroyed by the weight of the water on top of them. In contrast, gentle rain waters the flowers and stops them wilting in hot weather.

Activity – Show your child the garden after a heavy rainstorm and encourage him to try to prop up the squashed flowers so that they recover.

SEASIDE

Smells

Talk about the variety of smells that you might expect beside the sea. Mention seaweed, fish and chips cooking, barbecues, bonfires and so on.

Activity – As you walk along in a seaside town or on the beach, ask your child to tell you when he smells an unusual and different smell. Is it a pleasant or unpleasant smell? Can he tell you what it is?

Sounds

Listen out for all the different sounds at the seaside, for example, birds calling, waves lapping, leaves blowing in the wind, children shouting and laughing, motorboats, cars, ice cream vans and brass bands.

Activity – Can your child tell you what is making a particular sound?

Sailing boats

Look out for sailing boats of all different sizes. Watch how fast they go when there is a strong wind and how they gently float along when the wind is light. Explain that the wind catches the sails in the same way that it fills out and blows washing on the line. When the sail is full of wind, it pulls the boat along. Point out the boats' sails. Look at their size, shape and colour. Notice that many boats have more than one sail and the bigger the boat, the bigger the sails.

Activity – Together with your child, try making a model boat out of a piece of wood or plastic with some paper sails attached. Can your child tell you what shape the sails are?

Motor boats

Contrast the relative silence of sailing boats with the noise made by speedboats and jet skis. Watch these motorboats as they speed across the water. Again, there will be a vast difference in size and shape. Explain that these boats do not get pulled along by the wind, but have engines which drive them along very fast. These engines use petrol just like a car.

Activity – Buy a small wind-up boat or one that works with a small motor and encourage your child to play with this in the bath, listening to the noise and watching how the water is churned up by the action of the engine.

Anchors and mooring buoys

Show your child the boats in the harbour or sitting out in the bay. At low tide, many of them will be lying on the sand or mud and it is then possible to see the rope or chain which is attached to the boat and to an anchor, or to the boat and then a mooring stone and buoy. Notice all the different coloured mooring buoys which float on the water and show the boat owner where to go to be able to attach to his mooring. Explain that when the boat is sitting on the ground, there is no danger of it floating off, but when the tide comes in, something is needed to prevent the boat from floating out to sea. Explain the function of the anchor or mooring stone in terms of car and bicycle brakes or dog leads. Both these prevent the object from getting away.

Activity – Can your child help you to make an anchor to

keep his boat, or a plastic duck, where he puts it in the bath? Try making it into a mooring buoy by attaching a big, plastic bead to the main anchor rope.

Seabirds

Look out for seagulls, other gulls, terns, cormorants, kittiwakes and other seabirds. Point out the difference between the adult and baby seagull, in terms of colouring and size. Watch how some birds swim along and then suddenly dive for fish, staying under water for some considerable time, emerging with totally dry wings, as the water drops off their oiled feathers. Notice how others fly high in the air and dive into the water from quite a height, to catch their fish. Seagulls eat shellfish and often crack their shells by throwing or dropping them onto a hard surface. When the shell is broken, the bird can eat the soft fish inside.

Activity – Water drops off birds' feathers because they are very oily. When we get wet, the water sticks to us because our skin is not so oily. To illustrate the difference, let your child rub his hands with baby oil and then dip his hands in water. He will notice the water dropping off just like the seabird.

Look together at a book about seabirds. Talk about webbed feet and how this helps the birds to swim along fast. Look at the subtle differences in colour and shape of the various seabirds. Notice several common features – black and white colouring, long beaks, webbed feet, some orange or red markings somewhere.

Encourage your child to listen for the different cries of these birds.

Souvenir shops

Most children love to visit these shops. Before you take your child, ask him to tell you the sort of things they are likely to sell, bearing in mind where he is. Encourage him to think what people do when they are at the seaside. Talk about building sandcastles in the sand (buckets, spades and flags), fishing in rock pools (nets), playing games on the beach (bats and balls), going swimming (arm bands, towels and flippers) etc.

It is likely to be quite hot and sunny when most people come to the seaside. What will they need? Talk about sun hats, sun cream, ice creams and cold drinks.

Many people like to take back memories of where they have been and will therefore want to buy film for their cameras or coloured postcards of the area. When you visit the shop, encourage your child to make his own decision about a suitable purchase and to pay the shopkeeper himself.

Café

There will often be cafés at seaside resorts. These will obviously vary in size and in what they offer in the way of food and drink. Some will have waitresses who serve you while others will be self-service. Explain that if there are waitresses, you sit down at one of the tables, decide what you want from the menu and then tell the waitress, who will bring it to you.

In contrast, can he tell you what you have to do if it is a self-service café? Point out how all the food and drink is laid out behind a counter and you have to go and help yourself. At one end of the counter is a pile of trays. Show him how you take a tray and put what you want on this before you take it to the end of the counter in order to pay. Can he see where to get knives and forks, spoons and napkins? Can he find you an empty table to sit at?

COUNTRYSIDE

Hedges, fences and gates

Talk about hedges, fences and gates and why they are necessary in the countryside. Explain the need to keep animals enclosed, to avoid them escaping or causing damage. Tell him about the dangers of electric fences and why these are effective in keeping livestock in.

Activity – Let your child play with a set of farm animals, grouping them in separate fields and separating those fields with pretend fences and hedges made out of modelling clay or building blocks.

Farms and farmland

Look out for rolls or bundles of straw and hay sitting in fields. Watch farmers as they work on their land. In summer, look out for fields of grass being cut, using a mower behind a tractor. The cut grass will be left lying in the fields to dry thoroughly before being baled as hay, or it will be crushed and baled in plastic, for silage. Baling machines pick up the cut grass and quickly convert this to neat bundles. These bundles are stored and used during the winter for animal feed.

Watch out for crops of wheat, barley and oats which will be harvested using a combine harvester. This machine strips the grains from the crop and bales the remaining straw immediately into small square bundles or, more usually, large, round ones. Ask your child to watch carefully as the stripped stalks are thrown into the back of the machine before they appear again as neat bales. This straw is used for animal bedding.

Where might your child have seen a tractor? Explain that they are used for many jobs, including pulling ploughs to turn over the earth in fields before planting and for pulling heavy trailers.

Activity – If possible, watch a combine harvester at work. Ask your child to tell you what he thinks cows and horses eat. Explain that in summer, there is plenty of fresh grass for them to eat, but in winter, these animals need hay or silage instead. Bales of straw are used to provide them with soft bedding inside. Can he make a shed, using junk materials, for his farm animals to shelter in during the winter?

Features of the town and the country

Talk about the differences between the town and the country. Note how green the countryside looks in comparison to the town, due to the multitude of trees, fields and hedges.

Activity – Ask your child to paint a picture of the countryside and a different one of the town. Encourage him to think about what colours he uses most often.

Road signs
Look out for different road signs seen in the countryside, such as 'cattle crossing', 'railway crossing', 'deer', 'hump-back bridge' and so on.

Activity – Can your child tell you what these signs mean? Have fun guessing together. Let him design some of his own to be used with his toy cars. Can you guess what these mean?

Railways
Look out for trains crossing the countryside. Explain that to keep the track as flat as possible and therefore make the trains go faster, trains often cross the countryside on viaducts, bridges, cuttings or embankments. See if you can spot a viaduct as you go around the countryside. Point out how these are usually quite high up as they cross deep valleys. Bridges will be relatively easy to spot and will pass over rivers, roads, motorways and, occasionally, other railways tracks, allowing the train to cross these safely. Relate this to your child using a zebra crossing to cross the road safely. In rural villages, where there is relatively little traffic on the roads, look out for railway crossings, where the road is shut off only when a train is approaching. Look out for the flashing lights and closing gates. To avoid trains having to climb and descend steep hills, they often go through cuttings (which are below the surrounding ground) or on embankments (which are above).

Activity – Make an obstacle course together, using tables, chairs, play tunnels and anything else you may have around and have fun going under, over, around and through objects, pretending that you are a train on its journey. Take this opportunity to use lots of 'position' language.

Motorways

Talk to your child about these big roads and discuss the difference between them and a normal road. They help to get people to their holiday destinations as quickly as possible. When driving along, notice how many motorways go through country areas. As motorways are meant to be fast roads, the builders try to make them relatively straight. This means there will often be bridges and cuttings taking them over, under or through obstacles, just as there are with railway tracks. Point out bridges over the motorway, carrying other roads over the top.

Activity – Encourage your child to make some bridges out of construction kits, to go over and under an imaginary roadway made out of a narrow roll of paper (like that used for till receipts).

TOWN

Traffic

Most towns are now very busy with huge amounts of traffic, especially at peak holiday times. Explain the need to be very careful when walking out and about in town centres, to avoid being knocked down by cars, buses or lorries. What and who is controlling the traffic? Talk about traffic lights, which make cars and lorries stop and go at certain times. Also look out for police officers and traffic wardens who move cars along and prevent them from stopping where they should not be. Explain the need to keep certain areas free of stationary cars so that the traffic can keep moving. Point out that in this country, we drive on the left-hand side of the road, whereas, in many countries abroad, they drive on the other side.

Activity – Can your child tell you what other things police officers do? Take this opportunity to reinforce the fact that the police officer is his friend and that if he gets lost or separated from you, the police officer is there to help.

Maps
In unfamiliar towns, it may be necessary to look at maps to work out where you want to go. Show your child one of these location maps and point out some of the more obvious features of the town you are in.

Activity – When you get home, look together at various simple maps which have pictures to show the position of various features. Can your child help you to find the river, the cathedral, the castle?

Road signs
Look out for the various signs you are likely to see around the town, for example, 'school', 'road junction', 'roundabout' and so on.

Activity – Again, can your child guess what all the different signs mean.

Shops
Part of the joy of being on holiday in a town is to be able to go shopping. Notice how the biggest shops are normally all placed quite close together in the centre of the town so that they are easy for shoppers to get to. In many holiday towns, there will be tourist shops, selling souvenirs and many of the local specialities. Point these out.

Activity – Allow your child to have a little of his own money to spend. Can he explain what he wants to buy and hand over his money?

Tourist attractions
Towns present many opportunities for having fun on holiday, for example, sea-life centres, swimming pools, museums, zoos, cinemas and theatres. Facilities will vary

depending on the town, but most will provide a good selection. All will give you and your child endless opportunities for looking and learning and enjoying together. As well as the obvious attractions of each, watch out for interesting or unusual features. For instance, some swimming pools have imaginative flumes, consisting of a complex tangle of tubes. Many zoos now have amazing play areas for apes and monkeys. Don't forget to look at the actual building as well as what is inside, as some attractions are housed in unusual buildings. Cinemas and theatres offer a vast range of opportunities nowadays, with the arrival of 360 degree screens, to really involve the viewer. After each visit, encourage your child to think and talk about what he has seen or experienced.

VILLAGE FÊTES

Stalls
Give your child an opportunity to examine all the stalls – both those selling goods and those which invite participation in the way of a competition of some sort. Encourage him to take part by guessing how many sweets are in the jar, where the treasure is buried and by throwing hoops over his preferred prize etc. If you are involved in helping at the fête, make sure your child is included and encourage him to think of a different type of stall. What could you sell or make into a game?

Flags, balloons and signs
As you go round the fête, notice the various decorations and signs which have been put up. Why does your child think this is? Explain that the purpose of fêtes is to raise money for schools, churches, the village, etc. and the more people who come, the more money the fête will make. By making it look attractive, people will notice what is going on and be more likely to come in. The various signs show people where to go.

Bouncy castles

Can your child tell you what is inside the bouncy castle to make it so bouncy? Compare the feeling to squeezing a balloon which has been blown up to about half its capacity. Let him see you blowing air into the balloon so that he can make the connection to air being inside the castle. Why does he have to take off his shoes when he plays on it? What happens to a balloon when it is pricked? If he doesn't know, try!

...a balloon which has been blown up to about half its capacity.

Teas and ice cream

No doubt you will soon find yourself at the refreshment stall, particularly if it is hot. Explain that it is hard work walking round and having a go at everything and people need a rest and something to eat and drink. Encourage your child to make his own selection and pay for what he has chosen.

Fancy dress

There will often be fancy dress competitions at fêtes. It is usually possible to create something quite simple, even if your artistic talents are not all that great! Encourage your child to come up with suggestions and ideas as well and try to involve him in the making process. It is best to emphasise the fun of the event, because some outfits can be very hard to beat in a closely fought competition! Can your child guess what all the other competitors have dressed up as?

Dog show

If you have a dog, you may feel inclined to go in for this event. Either way, it will be a good event to watch. Look out for all the different breeds of dog in all shapes and sizes. Discuss together which animals he likes best and why. Which are the fiercest looking dogs? Which does he think are the most obedient/naughty and why?

Music

Listen out for music at the fête. You may hear brass bands or perhaps barrel organs. Spend some time watching, close to the music. What sort of music are they playing – happy or sad? Is the band wearing uniform? Notice that all instruments in a brass band are blown. Watch any movements on the barrel organ. Explain that there is a mechanism inside that plays the music, rather like a tape.

FAIRGROUNDS

Similarities to fêtes

Big fairgrounds have many of the same features as smaller fêtes. There will be stalls, competitions, music and so on. What are the major differences? Talk about a much bigger area, more people and the need to stay close to adults for safety. What noises can they hear?

Fairground lorries and trailers

These bring the rides and merry-go-rounds to the fairground site. Many of the rides have to be taken apart to fit on the lorries and then reassembled when they get to their destination. Look out for convoys of these lorries, especially in the summer holidays or near bank holiday dates.

Big rides

There are often huge rides at fairgrounds – big dippers and

so on. Some of these will not be suitable for very young children. Explain the growing tendency to have a height bar to indicate whether children are allowed or not. Can your child guess whether he is tall enough, before you reach the bar? If you cannot or do not want to ride, watch from a suitable distance as the cars zoom up and down or round and round.

Merry-go-rounds

Gentler and easier for young children are the various merry-go-rounds which have a number of objects to ride as the roundabout goes round and the objects move gracefully up and down. Discuss speeding up and slowing down. How does your child know when it is time to get off? What must he do when the ride is moving?

Bumper cars

How is this ride different from driving a proper car? Can your child tell you why they are called bumper cars?

Candy floss and hot dogs

Certain sights are very common at fairgrounds and candy floss and hot dogs are always on sale. What does your child think candy floss is made from? Explain that it is made from sugar which has been heated to a very high temperature to make it liquid and then whipped very hard, just as you would whip cream.

Activity – When you get home, let him watch you (from a safe distance) as you heat up a variety of foods, such as chocolate, butter and sugar to see that these things all change from solids to liquids when they get hot.

8

Learning When Out on Visits

AT THE LIBRARY

Arrangement of books in the library – different library sections

When you first go into the library, show your child the various signs which tell him where to find books about particular subjects. Point out the notices (animals, poetry, transport etc.) on the ends of the shelves and help him to read them. Bearing in mind what he is interested in, see if he can find the area of the library which will have books on this subject. Explain that books about similar subjects will usually be on shelves close to each other.

Activity – Encourage your child to find out new information about his favourite topics by looking at a variety of books and choosing some to borrow and take home.

Areas for book browsing

Look out for comfortable seating areas. Why do libraries have these? Explain the need for somewhere comfortable to sit while you look at the books you are interested in and decide which ones you want to borrow. Most libraries have child-size seats and sofas or bean bags. Show him how bean bags take up the shape of his body and form a comfortable moulding around him when he sits down.

Storage – book shelves and boxes

How are the books stored and displayed? Look out for shelves and book boxes. Can he see books very well when they are in the shelves? Point out that it is much easier for him to see exactly what sort of book he has found when he can see the whole cover, either in a box, or when propped open on top of a shelf. If the cover looks appealing, he can then investigate further by looking at the pages inside.

Storytimes

Many libraries have set storytimes when members of the library staff will read a selection of stories out loud to the children. To encourage his enjoyment of reading and books, try to include your child in some of these.

Activity – Be sure to continue reading to him at home.

Computers

Look out for computers in the library. Explain that these are used for keeping records of which books the library stocks and for checking whether books are available or out on loan. Many libraries also have a number of computers for use by members of the public. They will often provide suitable software to keep children interested and amused.

Exit

When your child is ready to leave the library, having chosen some books to borrow, show him where he has to go. Give the librarian your library ticket and let him see how she scans it so that a record of the books your child has borrowed are listed on the computer under his name. Watch as she uses the rubber date stamp to stamp the books. Explain that books can only be borrowed for a certain length of time and this date stamp tells your child when he needs to bring the books back.

Activity – Back at home, encourage your child to make his own books, which you can staple together. Let him use any rubber stamps you may have to check them in and out of his 'library'.

AT THE SWIMMING POOL

Smells
Swimming pools have their own distinctive smell, due to the chlorine. Can your child distinguish this smell from the smell outside? The water also tastes different because of the chlorine and should not be swallowed in any quantity. Explain the need for this disinfectant to keep the water clean because it is used by lots of different people.

Sounds
Pools tend to be noisy. Explain that this is because of the high ceilings and all the people. There are no curtains or soft furniture to absorb the noise and so noise echoes around the building.

Changing rooms
Point out the different areas for ladies' and men's changing. How can your child identify which is which? Show him the signs or pictures. What else can he see in the changing area? Some pools may have separate cubicles for changing, while others just have a communal room.

Lockers
When your child has changed into his swimming costume, he needs to lock away his clothes safely in a locker while he swims. Show him how the lockers work. Let him put a coin in the slot, before shutting the locker, turning the key and removing it. Often the key is on a band or safety pin. Can he tell you why this is?

Activity – Emphasise the importance of not turning keys in any lock without an adult being with him and saying he can. Explain what could happen.

Showers and toilets
Before entering the pool, a visit to the shower and toilet area is usually essential. Explain how to use the controls on the shower so that the water does not get too hot, but do

not allow him under the shower without checking the temperature first. Let your child experiment with the hot air drier in the toilet. Why does this dry his hands? What happens to the water?

Hair dryers
After swimming and showering again, show your child where he can dry his hair. This is likely to be operated again with a coin in the slot. Can your child get it working for you?

Adult and children's pools
Many swimming pools have more than one pool. Can your child tell you why this might be? Can he notice the differences between them? Point out such things as size and depth, by watching people in the pools. If people are standing in the water, what does this mean? If they are diving into the water, what does this mean? Look out for babies and children in one pool and adults in the other.

Flumes and water slides
Some pools have flumes and slides. Emphasise the safety factors here. Some of these flumes are slippery and steep and children slide down them quickly, ending up in the water with a big splash. Children need to be able to swim before they use them. Let your child watch as people emerge from the tubes.

Safety rules
Why are there lots of safety rules at pools? Talk to your child about the dangers of water and slippery surfaces. Discuss how easy it is to slip or to hurt oneself or someone else by bumping into them. Why must he not run by the side of the pool? If he can't swim, what must he have so that he is safe in the water? Talk about arm bands, rubber rings and foam supports.

Activities
1. At home, let your child experiment with things which

float and those which sink. When he has discovered that a stone will sink in water, try wrapping it in bubble wrap, securing it with waterproof tape and putting it back in the water, to demonstrate the effectiveness of air (for example, arm bands) in supporting the object so that it will float.

2. Enjoy the water and learn to swim. Why does he think this is important?

AT THE PARK

Swings

Ask your child what you have to do to get the swing to move back and forwards. Emphasise the need for making sure that nobody is in the way before you start the swing moving. Are all swings the same? Point out how some look more like boxes, with bars around them. Can your child tell you why this might be?

Suggest to him that some swings are designed for tiny children who might fall out, whereas others can be used by more grown-up ones. Make the link with cots and beds. When your child is happily swinging to and fro, stop pushing and let him see if he can keep himself moving by swinging his legs. He will probably not be able to do this very effectively and will therefore slow down after a time. However, point out how long the swing maintains its momentum.

Activity – Help your child to make a small pendulum, by attaching a small brick to the end of a light piece of string and hanging this from a door frame. Ask him to pull back the pendulum as if he was starting up a swing and then let it go. Watch as the pendulum swings to and fro for quite some time, gradually slowing down just like the swing.

Climbing frames

Watch as your child plays on this piece of equipment. Does

he explore all the possibilities for playing on it? Point out any features he hasn't noticed. Is the frame made of wood or metal?

See-saws

Before your child gets on the see-saw, emphasise caution and ask him what will happen if he tries to get on to the side that is up in the air (a) if no-one is sitting on the other end and (b) if someone else is already on the other end. What is needed before the see-saw can work? Explain the need for roughly equal weights on each end.

Activity – To explain the action of a see-saw more fully, encourage your child to play with a beam balance, using objects of contrasting weight so that he can see that a bucket full of feathers weighs roughly the same as one tiny brick etc.

Slides

Notice the very shiny surface on slides that allows your child to slide easily down it. If there are slides at several different angles, ask your child which one he thinks will make him go fastest. Is the slide steep enough to keep him travelling to the very end of the run-out of the slide?

Activity – Set up several ramps of varying steepness and encourage your child to experiment with toy cars to find out which ramp makes the cars go fastest. It should be easy to see that the steeper the slope the faster the car will go and also, the further it will travel at the end of the slope.

Bouncy rockers

What makes these rockers rock? When no one is on them, point out the huge springs underneath them. Does he have any toys with similar springs to make them bounce such as hanging, bouncing mobiles?

WHILE FEEDING THE DUCKS

Watching the ducks

Watch the ducks as they swim slowly along and then make their way quickly to the source of the food – your child's bread. Look at them nibbling at the bread with their big, flat beaks, scooping it up out of the water, picking it up off the ground (remind him not to get too close, as ducks' beaks can hurt) or diving into the water to pick it up from the bottom of the pond. Notice how the ducks can go under water for quite some time. Watch as they up-end themselves, with only their tail feathers visible. What happens to the water on their feathers as they surface again? Notice how they still appear to be dry. Why is this? Explain that duck feathers are very oily and the drops of water just slip off them, leaving the ducks completely dry.

Point out how ungainly ducks are on the land, as opposed to the water. Watch how they propel themselves out of the water onto the side of the pond or banks of the river and then waddle along. Show your child their webbed feet. Can he say why they need these for swimming through the water? Explain that ducks can walk and swim. What else can they do which we can't? Notice how they fly off if your child frightens them.

*...then make their way quickly to the source of the food
– your child's bread*

Activity – When you get home, encourage him to try pushing water along with his hands. He will not be able to do it with his fingers separated, but with them closed, which is like having webbed feet, he will be able to.

Feathers

Look at the duck feathers, pointing out the long wing feathers and soft downy ones on the underside of their bodies. What colours can your child see? Notice the different colouring of male and female ducks.

Activity – If you see any discarded feathers on the ground, take them home and let your child examine them carefully. Decide whether they are wing or down feathers. What happens to the feathers if your child strokes them in the wrong direction? Notice how the parts of the feather separate. Encourage your child to dip the feather in water and watch as the drops run off.

Watching the water

Notice what happens to the water, when the ducks are swimming. Watch the pattern that is made in the water behind them. Point out what happens when the ducks dive into the water. Notice the circular ripples that spread out from where the duck has dived.

9

Learning As You Go About
Your Daily Tasks

AT THE HAIRDRESSER

Scissors
Hairdressing scissors are different to ordinary ones your
child might use. Can he suggest any reasons why this might
be? What does he think the differences are? Consider
sharpness, size, weight. Notice how the hairdresser keeps
them safely in their own special pouch to protect them.

Capes
Look at the capes which people wear when they have their
hair cut. Why does your child think this is necessary? Talk
about the dual purposes of these. They keep clothing dry
and clean and they also prevent hair sticking to clothing.
Show him how small pieces of hair, while attaching
themselves to clothing, slip off nylon capes. Notice how
some capes just wrap over clothing whereas others have arm
holes.

Different shaped brushes/different diameter rollers
Look out for the little trolleys which hold the various
rollers, brushes and pins that the hairdresser may want to
use on people's hair. Why does your child think there are
rollers and brushes of different sizes? Talk about long and
short hair and show him how large rollers fall out of short
hair whereas small ones will grip. It is the same with
brushes. The hairdresser needs to dry short hair with a
smaller brush. Explain that rollers are used to make straight
hair curly. The wet hair is wrapped around the roller. When

the hair dries and the roller is removed, the hair has taken on the bend of the roller and comes out curly.

Different height chairs for adults/children
Many chairs used at hairdressers can be adjusted for height. Why does your child think this is? Explain the need for both the hairdresser and the client to be able to see in the mirror in front of the chair. Small children sit much lower in the chair and they therefore need raising up. An alternative is to pad the chair with cushions or towels.

Mirrors and hand-held mirrors for back view
Hairdressers are full of mirrors. Why is this? Some are fixed to the walls whereas others are hand-held. Show your child how he can see the back of his hair by having a mirror held up behind him as he looks at the mirror in front.

Back wash basins
Basins in the hairdresser look different. How are they different? Point out the dip in the edge of the basin which is designed for your neck, as you sit back against them. Explain that you sit back against these basins so that you can have your hair washed without shampoo getting into your eyes.

Activities
1. Compare washing hair at home with having it washed at the hairdresser. At home, you will probably use the mixer spray on the bath taps or perhaps wash hair while your child is in the bath. Is he leaning back or forward when you wash his hair? Which is more comfortable and why?

2. Let your child feel the difference between brushing wet and dry hair. Hair which has just been washed tends to be in a tangle and difficult to brush, whereas dry hair is much easier.

Dryers – hand-held and hoods
When hair has been washed and cut, it needs to be dried
and this is usually done with a hand-held dryer. However,
your child will probably notice some ladies having their hair
dried inside a hood. Explain that this is because hair which
is in rollers is much harder to dry and needs to have
constant heat for much longer.

Check-in desk
When you leave the hairdresser, you will need to pay at the
check-in desk. Explain that this is where staff make
appointments on the telephone and prepare people's bills
for them. You can also buy hairdressing goods here –
shampoo, hairspray, brushes and so on.

AT THE DRY CLEANERS

Tickets
Explain to your child that some clothes can be washed at
home, whereas others – especially adult ones – need to be
cleaned at a special shop because they cannot be washed
without damaging them. When you take clothes to the dry
cleaners, let your child see what happens. Watch as the
assistant pins a ticket onto the clothes and gives you a
matching one.

Bagged clothes
When you collect your clothes, show your child how the
assistants have hung the clean, pressed clothes on clothes'
hangers and sealed them in long polythene bags. Tickets are
attached to these bags and when you hand over the
collection ticket this will be matched with the ticket on the
bag, to make sure the assistant gives you the correct
clothing.

Dry cleaning machines and steam presses
In some dry cleaners, you may be able to see the dry
cleaning machines in which the clothes are cleaned. Show

him that these machines are much bigger than the washing machine your child will have seen at home and explain that the clothes are cleaned with a special liquid, not washed with soap powder. When the clothes have been dried, they are ironed using a steam press, which does the same job as an iron, but much more quickly. Look out for assistants using this.

AT THE SHOE MENDERS

Machines and tools

Shoes don't last for ever and will need mending when they have been worn for some time. Explain to your child that most shoes which need mending are likely to be adult ones, because children's feet grow very quickly and they soon grow out of shoes. This usually happens before holes appear in the soles.

When you take shoes to be mended, watch out for the machines and other tools which the shoe mender uses to remove broken heels or damaged soles and to replace them with new ones. Your child will probably have seen a hammer being used or he may have used a toy one himself. The shoe mender will definitely use one of these at some stage during the mending process. He will also use strong glue to stick on soles and a knife to trim off excess sole or heel, prior to using the finishing machine for grinding and polishing.

Tickets and bagged shoes

Explain that when shoes are taken in, you will be given a ticket to bring back when you collect them. When the shoes are ready they will be put into paper bags with a ticket attached, ready for the customer to collect. The tickets are matched up when the shoes are collected.

Key cutting machines

Often shoe menders can also cut keys. Point out these machines and watch as the machine cuts a new key to match the old one. Often, sparks are formed as the cutting takes place. The operator may wear plastic safety glasses to protect his eyes from any sparks or small pieces of flying metal. Listen to the grinding noise as the keys are cut.

Shoe polish and laces

As you are waiting to collect your shoes, look out for shoe polish and cleaners of all different types – creams, sprays, liquids – all in lots of different colours. There may well be other things for sale. Look at shoe trees. Can your child tell you the difference between those for men and those for women? You will also be able to buy shoe laces. Explain that these come in all sorts of lengths because shoes vary in size and some lace-ups have two sets of holes whereas others have three, four or even five. The more holes that need to be laced, the longer the laces have to be. Let him experiment at home. Many shoes are not fastened by laces. What else is used?

AT THE PHOTO LABORATORY

Processing machines

Whether these laboratories are within chemist shops or are shops on their own, look out for the huge machines which process the film you have brought in. Show your child how these machines transform your small roll of film into photographs and their negatives.

Activity – When you get home, show your child a strip of unimportant negatives, together with its corresponding photographs. Provide a good light source and see if he can see the similarities between the two. Can he tell you what is different about them? Explain that the negative is the same picture as the photograph, but where the photograph is dark, the negative will be light and vice versa.

Strings of negatives and stacks of photographs

Watch out for negatives hanging up to dry. They come out

of the machine in a long string and are then cut into short strips. Can your child see photographs coming out of the machine and sitting in racks before they are collected and put in the special folder that is given to you?

Examples of photograph enlargements
Look around the walls of the shop or area for examples of photographs in different shapes and sizes. Explain to your child that it is possible to have photographs made into several different shapes and sizes and these are examples of what is possible. It is increasingly common to have photographs processed onto CD, so that they can be seen on a computer at home. If you have this facility, let your child see what you have to do to access these.

Frames and photograph albums for sale
Many shops sell photograph frames and albums, films and other photographic equipment. If you are buying a frame, explain how you find one the correct size. Let your child help you.

AT THE PETROL STATION
Petrol pumps
Explain to your child that different cars use different fuel. Most cars now use unleaded fuel as this causes less damage to the world about us. Does your child know where the petrol is stored in your car? Take him to the back of the car and let him find the petrol tank cap. Hold his hand and let him watch as you fill up the tank. Point out the numbers changing on the display on the top of the pump, which shows how much fuel you have bought and how much it has cost you. Explain that when the tank is full, the pump on the nozzle stops automatically, to stop the fuel overflowing. When you go to pay, take your child with you. How does the assistant know how much fuel you have bought? Point out the number beside each pump and explain that you have to tell the assistant the number of your pump.

Petrol station grocery shops

There are often small shops attached to petrol stations, stocking basic grocery items, newspapers, flowers, wood and coal. Explain that they tend to stock items which are heavy and awkward to carry around (wood and coal), things people might want to take to friends they are visiting (flowers and chocolates) or things they might have run out of if they have been away for the weekend (bread and milk). Many also sell ice creams and sweets, maps and things for the car. Is there anything you need?

Car washes

Many garages have car washing facilities. Some provide a hand-held spray wash, while others have a car wash you drive through. Take your child with you when you go in one of these and let him see what happens as you drive up to the wash and insert your ticket. Watch the spraying water and point out how the big roller brushes clean the car as they rotate round and round. After the wash, there is a rinse and then air is blown over the car to dry it. Explain this process in terms of your washing machine or dishwasher. They wash clothes and dishes whereas this machine washes cars.

Explain this process in terms of your washing machine.

Air for tyres

Just as your child's bicycle needs to have air in its tyres, so
does your car. It is possible for you to blow up a balloon as
the rubber is very thin, but the rubber in car tyres is tough
and needs to have air forced into it under pressure. There is
a special machine to do this at garages. Let him watch as
you put extra air into your tyres. You cannot use air in this
machine to pump up bicycle tyres because it comes out too
fast. Show him how a bicycle pump works in a similar way,
but at a slower pace. When do tyres need to have more air
in them?

AT THE POST OFFICE

Queuing system and cashiers

Many main post offices have queuing systems with a number
of cashiers working. Explain how the system works and that
usually you will be directed to a certain cashier, either by a
recorded voice giving a number or by flashing lights and
signs. Point out the number by each cashier.

Weighing machines, stamps, letters and parcels

You will often go to the post office because you have a
parcel or letter to post. Normal letters and cards can be put
straight in a letter box, with a first or second class stamp
on. Explain that if the letters are heavy or if they are going
to another country, they need to be weighed to find out how
much they are going to cost to send and, therefore, which
stamps need to be put onto them. Post offices have special
weighing machines which do this job. Let your child put the
parcel or letter on the scales. When the cashier gives you the
stamps, let your child stick them on for you and post the
letter in the box or put the parcel in the bag on the counter,
ready for posting.

Goods for sale

There will usually be items for sale in a post office as well as
stamps. Can your child tell you what else you need when

you are writing letters or sending parcels? Talk about writing paper, envelopes, pens, wrapping paper and packing boxes. Can your child find these things for sale?

AT THE VET

Reception area
Look out for the different animals which might be taken to the vet – cats, dogs, rabbits, hamsters. How are they transported to the vet? Point out baskets, boxes and leads.

Surgery
Point out the table in the middle of the room, for examining the animals. The vet will probably be wearing a white coat, in order to protect his clothing. Look out for the various instruments he might use when making an examination e.g. stethoscopes and thermometers. Your child may also see bandages, pills and medicines stacked on the shelves. If your pet has to have an operation, explain that he will stay overnight in a special hospital, which may well be attached to the surgery, as he will need to be looked after all the time.

10

Learning When Travelling

Most children are taken on journeys to visit relatives and friends and to go on holiday. Nowadays, they are much more likely to be widely travelled as everywhere has become so much more accessible. Many will be used to travelling quite long distances. Journeys are ideal times to fire children's curiosity and to encourage them to think about what is going on around them. It stops them from getting bored and encourages safety.

JOURNEYS ON FOOT

Road safety

Why is it important for children to 'stop, look and listen' before they cross the road? Talk about busy roads, point out the traffic on the road as you walk along and note how walking along the pavement keeps you out of harm's way. If you need to cross the road, it must be done in a safe place and in the company of an adult.

Zebra crossings and pelican crossings

Does your child know what these are for? Can he point out the differences between a zebra crossing and a pelican crossing? Explain that when drivers see someone standing at a zebra crossing, waiting to cross, they should stop, whereas, at pelican crossings, vehicles and pedestrians are controlled by traffic lights. When it is safe to cross, there will be a picture of a green, walking man and when you must wait, there will be a stationary red man. Why can you hear a bleeping sound when it is safe to cross? Explain that this is necessary for those who cannot see and are relying on their other senses to tell them when to cross. How do people who cannot see know where is a safe place to cross? Point out the little bumps on the surface of the pavement which help those who cannot see feel where it is safe to cross. Let your child stand on these so that he can feel the difference between this surface and the surface of a normal pavement.

Traffic lights

Notice the positioning of traffic lights. Why are some of them up high? What does each colour mean drivers should do? Let your child watch the lights changing and notice the correct sequencing of the lights as they go from green to red and from red to green. Why is it necessary to have an intermediate light between the red and green ones? Explain the need for a period of slowing down before vehicles can come to a complete stop.

Pavements

Point out the various types of pavement – tarmac, paving stones and cobbles. Other than new tarmac pavements, most will show signs of cracking or gaps between paving stones or cobbles. If children do not look where they are going, these gaps and cracks can cause them to trip. Notice how tree roots can cause the surfaces of pavements to buckle and crack. Explain the extraordinary strength that roots have to be able to do this. Explain that pavements provide a safe place for people to walk at the side of the road. The edge of the pavement is called the curb and this is where you must wait when you want to cross the road.

Letter boxes

Ask your child to look out for the bright red letter boxes. Let him post letters into the box. How will he know when those letters will be collected and taken to the sorting office? Show him the plate on the front of the box with numbers that correspond to different collection times. If he has a letter which is too big to fit into the mouth of the box, what should he do? Where must he take big parcels? Try to watch the postman collecting letters into his sack at one of the collection times. Watch him unlock the front of the box, reach in to pick up the letters and lock up the door again.

CAR JOURNEYS

Encourage your child's observation skills by asking him to look out for various things he might well see when he travels in any of the locations below. Play a game, giving him one point for each thing on your list that he finds. How many points can he score?

...to look out for farms.

Journeys in the countryside
For a journey in the countryside, children could be asked to look out for farms, fields, tractors and farm animals. In country villages, they could look out for churches, pubs, post offices, post boxes, village greens and village ponds.

Journeys at the coast
During journeys at the coast, ask them to look out for the sea, cliffs, rocky and sandy beaches, souvenir shops, cafes, sailing and fishing boats, harbours and seagulls.

Journeys in the town

Town journeys give them opportunities to find shops, banks, churches, pubs, traffic lights, buses, zebra crossings, parking meters and the various markings on the road. Point out the white lines in the middle of the road, explain the different meanings of the different lines – single, double and dotted. Look at other traffic on the road. Are there more cars, more lorries or more vans?

BUS JOURNEYS

Bus stops

Notice where these are, perhaps close to shops or buildings of interest. Why is this? Point out that they are spaced not very far apart, so that wherever you are you do not have too far to walk. Explain that buses or coaches which are travelling longer distances often start from a bus station, where you can get buses to many different places, whereas you can only go to certain destinations from individual bus stops. Point out the canopies that cover many bus stops and the seating which is often provided. Can your child tell why these are needed?

Information displays

Show your child where you can find the information about buses going from that stop. It could be on an electronic screen mounted at the stop or, alternatively, printed on a board attached to the stop. Can your child read the number of the bus when it arrives? Point out that all buses have numbers and destinations displayed on them.

Single and double deckers

Point out the difference between single and double decker buses. Where are the stairs in the double deckers? Why does your child think we have double deckers?

Advertising on the buses

A number of buses these days are covered with

advertisements. Explain why this is an effective way to promote products. Where else has your child seen advertisements as you go out and about? Talk about advertising boards at the roadside and on the side of buildings.

Drivers and conductors

Point out the driver in his compartment. On some buses, there is only a driver, who also collects your ticket money as you board the bus, whereas on others there is a conductor who will do this job. Look at their uniforms.

Inside the bus

Why does your child think there are knobs attached to the roof of the bus? Explain that these are for hanging on to when you have to stand and the bus is moving. Show him the bell you have to press if you want the bus to stop at a request stop, while at the same time explaining that he mustn't touch it unless you have asked him to.

Automatic doors

Watch the automatic doors as they open and close at each bus stop. The driver activates them. On buses with conductors, there is sometimes an open platform, rather than automatic doors. Explain the need for extreme caution while getting off this kind of bus.

TRAIN JOURNEYS

Before going on a train journey, it is worth taking your child to watch trains, perhaps as they go under road bridges where you can stop on the pavement and watch them. Seeing a train approaching at speed along a straight section of track is quite a formidable sight and can be very exciting. Make sure you hold onto your child to reassure him, as he may be frightened. Listen to the noise of the two-tone horn as the train passes. Point out the tracks that the train travels along and the overhead wires of electric trains. This is a good opportunity to emphasise the importance of keeping well clear of railway tracks – they are not somewhere to play.

Station design
Point out the enormous buildings which are the main stations in big towns and cities. Many are very beautiful to look at. Make sure your child looks up as well as ahead of him as many stations have magnificent roofs. Compare these huge buildings with the much smaller country stations.

Buying tickets
Explain that, before you go on a rail journey, you have to have a ticket. These can be purchased at special areas of stations or at travel agents or on the internet. It is rather like buying anything else, except that you can't really see what you have bought until you actually travel on the train. On the train and sometimes at ticket barriers, the guard will ask to see your ticket to prove that you have paid for the journey.

Departure and arrival boards
How do you know where to go to catch your train? Explain that when you know where you are going and what time your train leaves, you can find out which platform it goes from by looking at the departure board. How do we know which platform is which? Show him the big number boards by each platform. Explain that platforms with consecutive numbers are next to each other. If you are standing by number 2, can he find number 3?

Waiting rooms
Why does your child think waiting rooms are called that? Explain that you sometimes have to wait for trains to come into the platforms.

Platforms and signals
Explain that big stations can have as many as twenty platforms, whereas small ones sometimes have just two. There will obviously be correspondingly more platforms, the

more trains pass through the station. The platforms must be long enough to accommodate the whole length of the train. The number of carriages can vary from one or two to twelve or more. Inter-city trains have many coaches so they need long platforms, whereas local trains are much shorter and can use smaller ones. Look out for train signals high up above the tracks. Explain that they work in the same way as traffic lights on the roads.

Guards and drivers
As you walk up the platform to board the train, try to take the time to show your child the driver in his cab at the front of the train. Can he identify any of the other staff on the train. Look out for uniforms and badges.

Train carriages
Look at the layout of the carriage. Notice how some seats are facing forwards, while others face backwards so that a table can be fitted between them. Why does your child think they need to have tables in the train? Where are the toilets? How do you know if the toilet is free? Point out the illuminated signs. Locate the doors of the train. Most are now automatically opened, rather than slam door.

Buffet cars and restaurant cars
What do you do if you are hungry or thirsty? Explain that you can get something to eat and drink in the restaurant or buffet car on express trains or from a trolley on small, local trains. The restaurant and buffet cars are special carriages, with small kitchens stocked with food and drink. You can sit in the restaurant car to eat a meal, whereas, in the buffet car, you collect your food from the counter before returning to your seat to eat it. Walking along the train to get to these carriages can be a wobbly experience. Make sure your child holds on carefully when he is moving around the train.

AIRPORTS AND AEROPLANE JOURNEYS

Airport car parks and airport buses

As you approach the airport, ask your child whether he can see the large P signs for the car parks. Can he tell you why they are labelled in this way? Notice that the car parks are some distance from the airport terminal. Explain that passengers who leave their cars in these places have to get a bus to the airport terminal. Can he spot an airport bus? How do they differ from other buses?

Different areas of the airport – for arrivals and departures

When inside the terminal, point out notices that tell you where to go for arrivals and departures. When you are leaving by plane, you must go to departures which may be identified by a picture of an ascending aircraft. When you are collecting someone from a plane, you must go to arrivals, which may be identified by a picture of a descending aircraft. Explain the significance of these pictures.

Baggage trolleys

If you are leaving on a plane and you have lots of luggage, you will want a baggage trolley. Can your child explain why it is easier to carry a heavy load on a trolley?

Check-in desks – tickets

When you reach the check-in desk, let your child help you to hand over the tickets and passports for checking. Let him watch the bags being weighed and labelled and show him how the luggage goes on a conveyor belt to the back of the desk. Explain what happens next.

X-ray security equipment

When you go through into the departure lounge, explain that you and your hand luggage have to go through the security system, so the security staff can check whether you are carrying something dangerous. Explain that some things,

119

such as gas cylinders, could catch fire when taken into the cabin of an aircraft, while others made of sharp metal could be dangerous to passengers and must not be carried in the cabin. The archway you pass through is able to tell if you are carrying anything metal and makes a loud noise if you are. The security staff will then do an extra check of your body to see where the metal is. Sometimes, it will just turn out to be metal on a belt or loose coins in your pocket. The luggage tunnel provides an X-ray picture of the inside of bags, just as an X-ray machine gives doctors a picture of the inside of your body. The security staff can then tell if there is something in your bags which should not be there. If they see anything they are not sure about, they may ask you to open your bags so that they can check further.

Airport shopping
While waiting to board the plane, you may well want to visit some of the shops which are always in airports. They are there because people often want to fill the time they spend waiting.

Moving walkways
Passengers often have to walk quite some distance between the shopping areas and the boarding gates, where they can get onto the plane. To make it quicker to get to these gates, there will often be a moving walkway between these areas. These are giant conveyor belts which carry people, rather than groceries. Make the connection with supermarkets and encourage your child to see the similarities. Caution your child about getting onto and off these staircases as it is easy to trip if you are not looking where you are going.

Aircraft – seeing bags being loaded
When you reach the boarding gate, boarding cards will be checked and you may go through a further security check before you board the aircraft. Let your child try to find the seat number by matching it to the one on the pass. If you are allowed to carry hand luggage, where does he think your hand luggage should be stored? Can he show you how to work the seat belt? Why do seats in planes have these?

Compare them to belts in cars and buggies.

If your child is sitting in a window seat, encourage him to look out of the window to see the wings of the aircraft, the jet engines and any vehicles moving around the airport. Can he see the baggage or the food being loaded onto the plane? Encourage him to look out for the little tractors pulling several trailers loaded with luggage. When these reach the plane, they are loaded into the plane's hold by airport staff. He might also see the metal boxes, carrying food and drink, being hoisted up to the doors of the aircraft.

Taking off

Before take-off, doors must be closed and everything stowed away. Explain that the doors are heavy and strong and have big locking handles on them – not keys. Before it is able to take off, the plane needs to be at the end of a long runway. The planes cannot be kept there because they would be in the way of other planes. Therefore it is necessary for them to drive slowly (taxi) to the right place. Can your child suggest why planes need to have a long runway to take off? Explain that they are very heavy and need to gain speed rapidly before they have enough energy to lift off the ground and go up into the air. Compare this to birds, especially swans and geese, taking off from water.

In the air – looking down

When airborne, if you are near a window, encourage your child to look out. If it is a cloudy day, the plane will be in cloud as it gains height, but will suddenly come out into the sunshine. Can your child explain this? Explain that as planes go higher and higher, they eventually rise above the level of the clouds. If it is a clear day, let him identify towns, cars, houses, castles, rivers, mountains – which might have snow on them – sea and ships. If you fly over an area he knows well, help him to identify prominent landmarks.

Landing

When it is time to land, the stewardess will tell you to return to your seats and to fasten seat belts. Why is this?

Ask your child to listen to the different sounds of the engine as the plane comes in to land, especially the roar of the engines as the wheels actually touch the ground and the brakes are applied.

Arriving in a new country

When you arrive in the new country, look out for unfamiliar surroundings and listen for a different language. What does your child notice that is especially different? It might be the climate, the different clothes people are wearing, unusual food to smell and taste or the strange language people are speaking. Make sure he uses all his senses to help him detect differences.

FERRIES AND JOURNEYS BY SEA

Car ferries

Look at the shape and size of the ferry and see whether your child can work out where the cars go. Explain that the cars remain on car decks whereas the passengers have to leave their cars and go to the passenger accommodation which is on higher decks. As you drive on to the ferry, explain that you are going over a metal ramp which provides a link between the land and the sea. The ferry comes close into the jetty but there is always a gap, which is bridged with this ramp. When all the cars are loaded on to the ferry, the ramp is lifted and the heavy doors to the ferry are closed before it puts to sea.

Passenger ferries

On passenger-only ferries, all the space is taken up with facilities for the passengers – seating, shops, restaurants, toilets, entertainment rooms and so on. Point out the metal ramp or stairway that you walk across to board the ferry.

Rough passages

If the weather is good and the sea is calm, you hardly notice that you are on a boat on the water. However, when it is windy and rough, the ferry can rock substantially. Let your child experience how rough seas can cause you to lose your balance, while keeping a careful eye on him and explaining the need for him to be careful when moving around the ferry in these conditions. Cars, lorries and vans need to be secured firmly when it is rough and there are special fixing belts, attached to the floor which also go around the car's wheels, to keep them in place.

Hovercraft and catamarans
There are hovercraft and catamarans for both passengers and cars. These provide a much quicker journey as they travel at a much faster speed. Explain that hovercraft actually skim over the surface of both water and land. They sit on a cushion of air. The rubber skirt is inflated as the craft prepares to leave and it collapses and deflates when it ends its journey. Catamarans are ships with two hulls, which cut through the water much more quickly than the single hull of a normal ship. Show your child a picture of these craft as you explain how they are different to normal ferries.

11

Learning While Watching Others At Work

Children are fascinated by watching others at work and will become quite absorbed in what they are doing. This chapter is full of suggested discussions to have with your children as they watch. If you provide a few simple props and dressing-up clothes, you will enable your child to imitate these workers and therefore, to understand their work more fully.

It is fully recognised that all jobs may be carried out by both men and women and any reference to gender refers equally to both men and women.

POLICE OFFICERS

Point out the very distinctive uniform worn by police officers, together with their hats and helmets. Often, the first thing your child notices will be the loud siren and flashing light of the police car or police motorbike. Explain that when police need to get somewhere in a hurry to help someone, or to get to the scene of a crime, they switch on their siren and the flashing light to warn other people to get out of the way. What colour is the flashing light? Sometimes it will be possible to watch the police as they direct traffic. Point out the signals they make with their hands. What does your child think these mean?

FIREFIGHTERS

Look and listen out for fire engines on their way to deal with a fire. Is their siren the same as the police car's? If you get a chance to see inside the fire engine, your child will be able to see the uniforms and helmets of the firefighters inside. The fire engines carry many heavy tools for the firefighters to use if they need to free people who are trapped at the scene of a fire. Can your child see ladders on the fire engine, for getting people out of tall buildings? As you pass fire stations, your child will often be able to see the fire engines lined up ready to go at a moment's notice. They are always left with their doors open so that the firefighters can make a quick getaway.

AMBULANCE WORKERS

Again, these workers have a distinctive uniform and a special vehicle with lots of medical equipment. There are special beds or stretchers inside the ambulance, so that people who are very ill or badly hurt can lie down. Ambulances also have a siren to let people know when they are in a hurry because they are carrying someone who needs to get to hospital quickly. Can your child imitate the sound of an ambulance and compare it with that of fire engines and police cars? When ambulances arrive at hospitals, they are able to drive right up to the door. Why does your child think this is?

POSTMEN

Explain what happens when you post a letter. It is first picked up by the postal van, then taken to the sorting office before it is given to the local postman for the area for delivery to the relevant address. Can your child identify a postman? Look out for these uniformed workers with their red trolleys full of letters and parcels. Note how they push the trolley around as they work their way down the street, delivering letters to each house. Watch how the trolley stops when left on a hill – it has its own braking system.

As you go past houses in the street, look out for the letter boxes in the doors. Are they all in the same position on the

*Notice some which are low down as well
as the more normal central position.*

doors? Notice some which are low down as well as the more
normal central position. Can your child suggest what might
happen to letters that are too big to be delivered through
the letterbox? Explain how these are taken back to the
sorting office, while a card is left at the house, telling the
owner where to collect them from. If you live in a country
area, point out the red postal van doing his rounds. Why
does the postman deliver to these houses by van?

MILKMEN

Many people now buy their milk in supermarkets, but some
still have it delivered to their door. Depending on where you
live, you may notice milk floats delivering directly to houses.
Watch how slowly they go. Are the milkman selling
anything else as well? Can your child tell you the difference
between milk delivered in this way and milk bought at the
supermarket? Point out the glass bottles, in contrast to the
cartons or plastic bottles bought in shops. Because the milk
is delivered in glass bottles, the milkman has to collect the
empty bottles as well, so that they can be washed and used
again.

WAITRESSES

Many waitresses will have uniforms, but these will vary
according to the restaurant or café you are in. When you go
into a restaurant or café, explain to your child that they serve
a variety of food which is written on the menu. When you
have decided what you would like to eat, the waitress comes
to your table to take your order. She will write it down on a
pad and take it to the cooks in the kitchen at the back of the
restaurant. When it is ready, she will bring it out to you. See
if your child can order his own food, when you have told him
what is on the menu. Why does your child think the waitress
is wearing uniform? Before your child eats or before the
waitress brings food to you, what should they both do? Talk
about hygiene issues surrounding food.

ICE CREAM SELLERS

In summer, these vans are a common sight on our streets.
How can you tell if one is nearby? Talk about the jingles
they play. Each van has a special motor to keep the ice
cream cold. How can your child tell what kinds of ice cream
are for sale? Point out the poster at the front of the van
which has a picture of all the different varieties.

SUPERMARKET DELIVERY WORKERS

A more familiar sight in urban areas, these workers are
delivering goods bought in the supermarket to people's
homes. They bring the goods in special vans, with the name
of the supermarket on the side. The customer's goods are
packed into carrier bags by the supermarket and then
labelled with the customer's name. When you have your
goods, explain that you have to sign a receipt to show that
everything has arrived safely. Involve your child in
unpacking the bags. He will notice different labels on the
bags – chilled, frozen and ambient (room temperature),
probably in different colours. Explain what these mean and

let him put the chilled food in the fridge and the frozen, in
the freezer.

SHELF STACKERS

Supermarket shelves start the day full. Can your child tell
you what happens during the day as more and more people
come in to shop? After a while, the shelves need re-stacking
with new goods which have been delivered to the shop.
Point out the men and women who are doing this job. They
wheel huge trolleys, loaded with goods, to the relevant area
of the supermarket and stack the items onto the correct
place on the shelves. Very often, the goods come packed
into cardboard boxes and these have to be opened and
unpacked. Watch as stackers dismantle the boxes to make
them flat. Why do they do this and what happens to them
when they are dismantled?

Activity – Let your child help you to dismantle any
cardboard boxes you wish to dispose of, ready for recycling.

TICKET INSPECTORS

When you are travelling, by whatever means of transport,
you must have a ticket and the ticket inspector's job is to
make sure that you do. He comes along the train or bus
and looks at everyone's tickets to make sure they have paid.
Explain to your child that you must show him the ticket
when he asks to see it. He will then punch it with a special
tool to show that he has seen it. Show your child the little
hole made by the puncher.

Activity – If you have a hole punch at home, which works in
the same way, let your child play with it, making little holes
in scrap paper.

TRAFFIC WARDENS

Watch as wardens patrol up and down the street, pausing now and again to check car windscreens. Explain that they are looking out for tickets and permits because in certain areas, you have to have these in order to be allowed to park your car there. In certain other areas, you are not allowed to park at all. It is the traffic warden's job to write out and attach parking tickets to cars which are parked illegally. Tell your child what this means you have to do and how you can avoid getting a parking ticket in the future. Look out for parking bays, outlined in white and the machines where you can buy the tickets you need for parking. Explain how these work and show your child how to put money into the machine and watch the ticket being printed out. Show him where it tells you how much money to put in for a certain length of time. Let him stick the ticket on the windscreen of the car. Why does he think this is a good place to put it?

REMOVAL MEN

Explain the job of removal men. Show your child the huge vans that these men drive. Can he suggest to you why they are so big? What has to go in them? Notice the ramp leading up to the back of the van to make it easier to get furniture in and out. Look at the huge locking doors at the back. Notice the steps up to the very high driver's cabin. Removal men usually work in groups of at least three, because it is such heavy work. Watch them carry furniture in and out.

CRANE OPERATORS

Most cranes will seem huge to small children, and, therefore, fascinating. Watch how the crane arm lifts heavy objects into place, with the operator controlling the movement of the crane's arm from his cabin. Point out the heavy counter-balance weights, explaining this in terms of a seesaw, which needs balancing weights on each end to keep it level. Why are cranes needed to move large, heavy objects? Why are the workers around a crane all wearing strong helmets on their heads?

TELEPHONE ENGINEERS

Show your child how some telephone wires are carried on tall telegraph poles, although more and more are now buried under the ground. If something goes wrong with the phones, where lines are carried on poles, the engineer has to climb up to the wires and mend them. Point out how he has a safety wire attached to him, so that he cannot fall and a helmet to protect his head. Can your child see how the engineer climbs the telegraph pole? Show him the little steps all the way up.

WINDOW CLEANERS

Those who clean office-block windows will be seen in their cradle, high up on the side of buildings. Talk about safety harnesses and helmets. Those who are cleaning windows on smaller houses will be seen up ladders with their buckets and sponges. Point out that great care is needed on ladders, to avoid accidents. Notice the special tools that most window cleaners use. They first sponge the windows with soapy water and then remove the drips with a squeegee tool. Some will also have some sort of scraper for removing spots of paint and other hard spots that have dried onto the window. Can your child tell you why windows get so dirty, especially in cities?

ROAD SWEEPERS

Sadly, this is still a very necessary job. Rubbish collects on the streets because litter is still dropped by a lot of people. What should your child do with his litter? Point out litter bins in your area. If there are no litter bins, for example at stations, what should he do? Notice the special tools – a firm brush, long pincers and a long-handled dustpan, for lifting and sweeping up rubbish, without having to bend down. They also have a bin on wheels, into which they can empty their dustpans when they are full. Notice how the rubbish tends to be blown into the gutters at the side of the road. The road sweeping job is now often done by motorised vehicles, which have revolving brushes which collect the rubbish into the body of the machine.

REFUSE COLLECTORS

This is another messy job so the collectors tend to wear overalls to cover up their clothes. Again, they may wear bright orange garments over the top of their overalls in order to make sure that they are easily seen by other road users, while they pick up everyone's dustbins. They usually wear thick, rubber gloves. Can your child tell you why?

Watch as the dustbin lorry moves slowly along the road, stopping frequently to pick up dustbins and emptying these into the back of the lorry. After several dustbins have been emptied, the driver operates the crushers at the back of the lorry and these push the rubbish into the very back of the hold, leaving room at the front, for the next lot of rubbish. Blocks of flats have very large dustbins on wheels and these are lifted and emptied into the lorry mechanically. Can your child tell you why these cannot be lifted?

Make sure he notices the flashing orange lights on the top of the lorry as it moves along the road and understands the significance of the bleeping sound which he can hear whenever the lorry reverses. Why is it important to listen out for this?

BUILDERS AND PAINTERS

It is often possible to watch builders and painters at work. As it is a messy job, they often wear old clothes. Watch painters use scrapers, blow torches and sanders to make surfaces clean and smooth before they start painting. Notice how they use big brushes and rollers for large areas and much smaller ones for windows and doors. Look out for cement mixers, mixing cement for sticking bricks together when builders are constructing new walls. They will often need to use pulleys to get heavy tools and materials up to roofs and onto scaffolding. You may see a skip next to building work. Can your child tell you what this is for?

SCAFFOLDING WORKERS

Explain that buildings need to be repainted from time to time and work needs to be done to roofs, to stop them leaking. When builders and painters need to get up high to work on buildings they often have to use scaffolding. Scaffolding is rather like a climbing frame, but only for adults to use, as it can be dangerous. Watch as they construct this from huge metal poles and long planks of wood. They start at the bottom and climb onto what they have already constructed in order to make it higher. Look out for dustbin chutes for sending rubble from the top of a building to the bottom. Why are these workers using helmets? What special tools do they need to put the scaffolding together?

ROAD MENDERS

Explain that road surfaces do not last for ever and they eventually get holes in them, just like the soles of our shoes. Look out for the orange cones and road signs, which indicate 'road works'. Again, there will probably be a group of workers working on a particular job together. Look out for a number of lorries and vans carrying tools and equipment and large road rollers, used for flattening the new road surface after it has been mended. You may also see shiny, new, black tarmac being laid and melting, steaming pitch being used to mend the road's surface. This is a messy job too and workers will often be wearing old clothes or overalls. Why does your child think the workers wear bright orange waistcoats over their clothes? Look out for workers laying gas and water pipes at the same time.

JCB OPERATORS

On new building sites or major road improvement sites, you will often see JCB diggers in operation. Notice how they can move earth from one place to another, to make room for a new house or road. The operator sits in his cab and manipulates the 'bucket' so that it grabs a bucketful of earth. He then swings the arm of the JCB, so that the earth can be dumped somewhere else. The bucket can also be used for smoothing the dumped earth in its new location. Show your child how the look of a site can be transformed dramatically in quite a short time, with the use of these machines.

12

Learning to Get On with Others

Learning to get on with other people as we grow up is a fundamental need and is another vital learning skill. What are the key elements?

Being aware of others and recognising feelings

Most young children are very self-centred and they have to learn to think about others and to be aware of their feelings, as well as their own. This takes time. If your child is to become sensitive to the feelings of others, he will need to be able to recognise and express those feelings in himself. Therefore, it is very important not to ignore feelings in your child. Reflect what he might be feeling by talking about it, recognising that children may feel very strong one day, only to feel very vulnerable the next.

> *'I can see you are very happy because . . .' or 'I wonder why you are feeling so happy at the moment?' 'You must be feeling very frustrated because. . .', 'I can see you are angry. Tell me about it.' 'You seem worried. I wonder why?'*

This will help him to show empathy towards others. It is not easy for a young child who is feeling very aggrieved for whatever reason, to think about how another child might be feeling. Consider the reactions of a child who is unable to have the toy he wants because someone else has it. He has to be taught to think about how the other child might feel if he were to have it taken away. How can he resolve this awkward situation satisfactorily? It is only by experiencing positive outcomes to his actions that he will gradually be able to accept that it is better for him to behave in certain ways than in others.

Let us take the example of the toy. If your child snatches the toy, as he would almost certainly naturally do, the other child is very likely to protest strongly and the two of them may well get into a 'tug of war' situation. This will make no one happy and is certainly not a positive outcome. However, if your child can be distracted with another toy, he will still have something to play with and will not have to face a hostile playmate. Explaining that it would be unkind to take away a toy another child is playing with will gradually help him to learn how to consider others. If, at the same time, you tell him that once the other child has finished playing with the toy in question he can have a turn, he is more likely to be able to cope with a potentially very difficult situation. Instead of a negative outcome, you now have the beginnings of a positive one.

Understanding others

Understanding what makes others tick, or being able to put yourself in someone else's shoes, is a vital skill and only comes with time and practice. One of the most important factors in learning to understand people is to listen carefully to them and also to watch their reactions in certain situations. By doing this, the individual characters of various children become clearly evident. Understanding that some children feel threatened by certain situations and are not naturally as brave as others is important if children are to incorporate others successfully into their play. Realising that there is a need for both leaders and followers is essential if children of substantially different characters are to benefit from each other.

Showing tolerance towards others

Sometimes, we seem to be living in an increasingly intolerant society. There are an increasing number of news stories about clashes between people of different ethnic origins and different values. Therefore, when children are young, it is important to explain the values of all members of society and to explain why everyone is important. It is also important to discuss why differences enrich society and why everyone is capable of contributing much to the world and should therefore be greatly respected. Without the ability to show tolerance towards one's fellow human beings, life is bleak.

Displaying flexibility

From birth, children are very demanding and completely inflexible. Gradually, at a few months old, they can cope with slightly less strict routines and with being moved from place to place or having their meals at slightly different times. This flexibility in their daily routine continues to grow as they get older, but will never become completely flexible. Therefore, it is understandable that children find it hard to be flexible in other areas of their lives. They are used to reacting in certain ways to certain situations and will therefore continue to do so unless encouraged to do otherwise. It is a parents' role to help their children to show more and more flexibility as they grow up and to begin to respond in more appropriate ways to things they find difficult. Take the example of the contested toy described above. The pre-programmed response is to snatch the toy. A more adult, and more flexible approach could be to ask to share the toy or to offer the other child something else, in the hope that they might be prepared to give up the toy your child wants.

Accepting responsibility

Young children are unwilling to accept any responsibility in conflicts involving other children. They see the situation totally in terms of them having being 'wronged'. Again, it takes time and considerable help from you to accept that they could perhaps have done something differently which might have stopped the situation from getting as difficult. While it may sometimes be easier just to side with your child, it is actually important to discuss with them what happened and to make them think about their role. By doing this, you will help them to see the situation in a more balanced way, from both parties' points of view.

Being friendly, kind, polite and helpful

One of the crucial elements to getting on with others is to
be friendly. It is much easier to respond warmly to those
who are naturally friendly. Encourage your child to smile
and to be welcoming. Praise him for being kind and helpful,
provide him with lots of interesting and exciting activities to
keep him busy and let him enjoy life. This way, he will have
plenty to feel happy about and will find it easier to respond
happily to others. Encourage him to be polite and praise
him when he remembers to say please and thank you. Give
him practice in having conversations with other people. Talk
to him, keeping any questions as 'open' as possible (those to
which the answer is not just 'yes' or 'no') and encourage
him to ask and respond to questions by himself, so that he
gains confidence.

Activities – role-play

1. Explain to your child what you want him to do. You will
   pretend to be the shopkeeper and your child will come
   to the 'shop' to spend his pocket money. Ask him to ask
   you to help him. Role-play two scenarios. In the first,
   greet your child in an unfriendly way, with a frown on
   your face and by using a grumpy voice. When he asks
   for your help, respond in an unhelpful way. In the
   second, welcome him to the shop with a smile on your
   face and invite him to look around. Use a gentle,
   encouraging voice. Give help willingly. Which shop
   would your child rather go to? Can he explain to you
   why? Reinforce the importance of the qualities of the
   second shopkeeper and encourage your child to adopt
   these qualities as part of his character.

2. To help your child to understand others, encourage
   careful observation of others and careful listening to
   what they are saying and how they are saying it. Start by
   asking your child to try to identify a series of facial
   expressions that you will make – including an angry face,
   a happy one, an excited one, a sad one, a bored one and
   any others you can think of. Can your child identify

them? Next, put a blindfold on your child and see if he can identify the feelings by simply listening to your voice as you say a very simple sentence in a variety of tones. Emphasise the importance of these two senses as he tries to understand others and work out the best way of relating to them.

Concentration on these key elements will help your child to learn how to get on with others.

The aim on this book has been to help you to teach your child how to learn.

GOOD PROGRESS CHECKLIST

- Is your child pointing things out to you and is he getting excited by his discoveries?
- Can he tell you how he is feeling?
- Are you having fun together?

Further Reading

Bright Child, Dr Richard C. Woolfson (Hamlyn)

Entertaining and Educating Young Children, Robyn Gee (Usborne Publishing Ltd)

Montessori Play and Learn, Lesley Britton (Vermilion)

More Quick Fixes for Bored Kids, Tommy Donbavand (How To Books)

The Parenttalk Guide to Great Days Out, Steve Chalke (Hodder and Stoughton)

Raising Happy Children: What Every Child Needs Their Parents to Know, Jan Parker and Jan Stimpson (Hodder and Stoughton)

Quick Fixes for Bored Kids, Tommy Donbavand (How To Books)

Raising the Successful Child, Sylvia Clare (How To Books)

Releasing Your Child's Potential, Sylvia Clare (How To Books)

The Secrets of Successful Parenting, Andrea Clifford-Poston (How To Books)

Your Child at Play, Marilyn Segal (Vermilion)

When Your Child Starts School, Su Garnett (How To Books)

Web Sites

The Good Web Guide for Parents, Harriet Griffey (Good
 Web Guide)

forparentsbyparents.co.uk
www.itson.co.uk (a directory of useful sites)
www.ukparents.co.uk
www.familiesonline.co.uk
www.practicalparent.org.uk
www.preciouslittleones.com/uk

Index